Finding Our Way

A Guide to Adult Educators

Dedication

I dedicate this book to Laurence Robert Cohen who has guided and supported my writing, thinking, and learning about teaching.

Finding Our Way

A Guide to Adult Educators

Patricia Cranton

Wall & Emerson, Inc.

Toronto, Ontario • Dayton, Ohio

Orders for this book or requests for permission to make copies of any part of this work should be sent to:

Wall & Emerson, Inc.
Six O'Connor Drive
Toronto, Ontario, Canada M4K 2K1
Telephone: (416) 467-8685
Fax: (416) 352-5368
E-mail: wall@wallbooks.com
Web site: www.wallbooks.com

Layout and design of text and cover: Alexander Wall

National Library of Canada Cataloguing in Publication Data

Cranton, Patricia
    Finding our way : a guide to adult educators / Patricia Cranton.

Includes bibliographical references and index.
ISBN: 1-895131-23-5

1. Adult education. 2. Teaching. I. Title.

LC5215.C733 2003   374'.13   C2003-903713-4

Printed in Canada.

About the Author

Patricia Cranton received her B.Ed. degree (1971) and M.Sc. degree (1973) from the University of Calgary and her Ph.D. degree (1976) from the University of Toronto. Patricia's primary research interests have been the evaluation of teaching in higher education, instructional development, and transformative learning. She was selected as an Ontario Distinguished Scholar in 1991 in recognition of her research and writing on teaching and learning in higher education. She received the Ontario Confederation of University Faculty Association's Teaching Award in 1993 and the Lieutenant Governor's Laurel Award in 1994 for an outstanding contribution to university teaching.

In addition to her numerous articles and conference presentations, Patricia Cranton's books include *Planning Instruction for Adult Learners* (1989) with a second edition in 2000, *Working with Adult Learners* (1992) also translated into Japanese in 1999, *Understanding and Promoting Transformative Learning* (1994) also translated into Chinese in 1995, *Professional Development as Transformative Learning* (1996) nominated for the Cyril O. Houle award, *No One Way: Teaching and Learning in Higher Education* (1998), *Personal Empowerment through Type* (1998), and *Becoming an Authentic Teacher* (2001). Patricia has edited three New Directions volumes, *Transformative Learning in Action* (1997), *Universal Challenges in Faculty Work: Fresh Perspectives from around the World* (1997), and *Fresh Approaches to the Evaluation of Teaching* (2001).

Patricia Cranton's current research is a federally funded exploration of how faculty in higher education develop as authentic teachers.

From 1976 to 1986, Patricia Cranton was at McGill University in the Centre for Teaching and Learning and the Department of Educational Psychology and Counselling. From 1986 to 1996, she was at Brock University in the Faculty of Education. She founded Brock University's Instructional Development Office and directed it from 1991 to 1996. From 1996 to the present, Patricia has worked as an independent educator and writer. She recently completed a contract at the University of New Brunswick and is now a Visiting Professor at Saint Francis Xavier University.

Table of Contents

Preface

It is generally agreed that student transformation and development are the primary goals of adult education. Whether we are teaching basic literacy skills, training tradespeople, helping adults returning to school adjust to the new and bewildering environment, or working with teachers in a graduate level seminar, we are helping adults transform and develop. Providing people with information and technical skills has as much power to transform lives as does fostering self-awareness or overcoming anxiety about learning. In today's world, a person who has poor reading and writing skills or lacks the expertise to access the internet is as handicapped as someone who cannot function in a team environment or holds narrow and prejudicial views of other cultures.

I have come to see the different kinds of knowledge as forming a spiral, each one necessary to adult learning. Instrumental or technical knowledge forms the foundation from which students work. Its acquisition enables people to gain communicative knowledge—the knowledge of ourselves, others, and the social world in which we live. Its acquisition also enables learners to become free from the constraint of not knowing or not being able to do something—emancipatory knowledge. Emancipatory knowledge in turn allows people to obtain further technical and communicative knowledge.

Adult learning is said to be of four general kinds. We acquire new knowledge. We elaborate on or add to existing knowledge. We transform assumptions and beliefs that were previously absorbed without questioning. We transform perspectives or worldviews. However, it is *through* new knowledge that it becomes possible to transform and develop—transformation does not come out of nowhere. Therefore, all of the work we do as adult educators has the potential goal of transformation.

The literature on learning as transformation and adult development

ADULT LEARNING IS NOT A BOOT CAMP.

provides solid theoretical descriptions of these important processes. Good research has been conducted within the last decade to help us understand how adults engage in transformative experiences. Participation at international conferences on transformative learning has increased dramatically, and valuable discourse now takes place among scholars in this area. But when it comes time to teach teachers how to foster transformation and development in their classrooms, the resources are rare. Year after year, in courses, seminars, and workshops, educators challenge me with, "Yes, but how exactly do we *do* this?"

In this book, I present a series of concrete, practical strategies for the adult educator who is interested in promoting student transformation and development. The strategies are based on my experience and the theory and research in the area, but I do not write about the theory. The underlying theoretical models are mostly invisible. The sequence of chapters roughly follows the usual sequence of a course or workshop, beginning with getting to know the participants and ending with the last class of a course or the last hour of a workshop. It is my intent that such a structure will facilitate access to the information as it is needed, as well as create a logical order for the reader who likes to go through a book from beginning to end.

The chapters are short, each having one focus, such as setting up discussions, asking questions, or designing learning activities. Each chapter follows a consistent format. I introduce the purpose of the chapter, often with an illustrative story from my own practice. I then describe various strategies and techniques to achieve that purpose. This format leads to a detailed, practical guide to helping adults learn. There is a delicate balance between prescribing what educators should do and being true to the complexity of the teaching and learning process. The decisions about what to do in the classroom depend on the nature of the learning, the context, the students, and the teacher himself or herself. Yet, it is natural enough for educators to expect to find some answers when they pick up a book on teaching. I use my experience, both in terms of my own teaching and my writing about teaching, to walk that fine line between presuming to be able to tell someone else what to do and providing helpful advice based on expertise.

Although the context within which adult educators practice obviously influences what they do, I believe that the essential process of helping adults learn is common across settings. The book is addressed to educators in a wide variety of settings including colleges and universities, continuing education, web-based learning, human resource development in organizations, and more informal learning settings. Anyone who teaches adults anything should find the book useful.

Purpose

The purpose of this book is to provide a comprehensive and practical guide for educators who want to help adults learn. My objectives are to provide direction for adult educators in the following areas.

- Starting out a new course or workshop, including how to set up the room, introduce the session, demonstrate our own teaching values, and help people get to know each other.
- Setting up the learning environment to be supportive, challenging, performing, reflective, or some combination of these climates.
- Creating opportunities for participants to have input into and make decisions about their learning by selecting topics, strategies, resources, and learning projects.
- Fostering student responsibility for learning by being a co-learner, leaving students alone, asking rather than telling, and encouraging students to teach each other.
- Understanding learning styles through psychological-type preferences.
- Establishing relationships with students that are respectfully distant, collegial, or close.
- Organizing sessions by using an agenda, providing an overview, having a good introduction, changing pace, allowing natural flow to occur, clarifying relationships among topics, and ending well.

- Managing time when we are presenting material, leading discussions, and facilitating group work.

- Selecting readings, deciding on how much reading, making a decision about a textbook, using readings to challenge points of view, and reflect the diversity of the group, and using alternatives to academic readings.

- Setting up and facilitating discussion, dialogue, and conversation.

- Getting feedback from participants, including both informal and more systematic comments, and learning how to use and respond to feedback.

- Creating variety by changing the people, the media, the setting, the content, and the nature of the interactions among people.

- Being authentic and bringing our genuine selves into our teaching.

- Using group work including forming effective groups, being aware of how groups develop over time, considering the room set-up, giving good directions, and having groups report back.

- Designing learning activities for in or outside of the classroom—activities that encourage people to think, question, reflect, and become open to alternative points of view.

- Challenging and supporting student learning and knowing when to do each.

- Using technology in teaching, including e-mail, discussion forums, web boards, and online learning.

- Asking questions that encourage each of the four kinds of adult learning—acquiring new knowledge, elaborating on existing knowledge, transforming assumptions, and transforming perspectives.

- Giving informal feedback, providing students with meaningful written comments, and using personal interviews.

- Creating opportunities for individuation by helping students become aware of, separate from, and join collectives.

- Giving meaningful evaluations for each of instrumental, communicative, and emancipatory learning.

- Ending a course or a workshop in a meaningful and appropriate way.

Chapter One

Starting Out

Many years ago, when discipline was a schoolteacher's primary concern, new teachers were advised to establish immediately their authority over the class, to be firm, if not stern, to impose order right from the start. I remember a young teacher who entered our high school science classroom shouting and blustering on the first day, slightly red in the face from the exertion of establishing his role as disciplinarian. We never did take him very seriously. Although I assume those days are over, that advice did contain a kernel of truth. What we do at the very start of a course or workshop goes a long way toward establishing the nature of the learning experience for everyone involved, students and teacher alike.

If we want students to learn, they must be interested in the class or course material and believe that the learning will be relevant to their own personal or professional goals. If we want students to discuss issues, they must feel free and comfortable in speaking to each other. If we want students to be curious and questioning, they must be sure that questions are welcome. Although these ideas seem obvious, educators can easily forget them in their desire to cover the course material.

Attract interest

The opening of a workshop or training session or the first class of a course is the ideal time to pay attention to these issues. In this chapter, I discuss starting-out strategies, including how to set up the room and how the educator's position in the room influences students' perceptions, how to introduce the session, how to present our own values and show respect for students, and how to break the ice among a group of strangers. I include two examples of introductory activities that may be helpful.

Selecting the Room

We rarely have any choice in the room available for teaching or training. Sometimes space is limited. Often, people well removed from the educational process itself are in charge of things such as rooms and scheduling. However, if we do have a choice, here are several points to consider.

- Are the chairs (and tables, if appropriate) comfortable and moveable?

- Does the room have good lighting?

- Is there access to refreshments for breaks?

- Is there air conditioning for summer sessions?

- What is the noise level in the hallways or outside of the windows?

- Are whiteboards, blackboards, overhead projectors, LED projectors, computers, or other equipment available and working?

- Are all specialized requirements met, such as access to laboratory space, working machinery and tools, or supplies specific to the content?

- Is all this organized in advance? Otherwise, it's a good idea to ask someone to check on these small but crucial details.

Setting Up

In adult education, a circle of chairs and tables is traditionally used as a means of encouraging people to talk directly to each other. There are some objections to the circle formation: people may feel vulnerable or obligated to participate when everyone is looking at them. However, I find that a circle does tend to foster good communication and equality in participation.

- I always go early to my classroom and set up a circle before people arrive.

  However, if the group is larger than 20 or 25 people, a circle is less effective.

- An alternative is to arrange groups of tables and chairs that allow five or six people to sit together.

Other small things can have an impact on the way the room, and hence the learning experience, are perceived by participants.

> I personally do not think that adult students should ever sit in rows facing the front of a room. Such a set-up not only discourages people from talking to each other by forcing them to turn around to see behind them, but also establishes a clear power position—the front of the room usually occupied by the teacher.

- Clear away all traces of previous occupants, such as writing on a whiteboard, chart paper on the walls, or even empty coffee cups and apple cores.

- Stack unused tables and chairs neatly out of the way.

- Arrange chairs or desks in preparation for the session to come.

- Have illustrative material such as charts or handouts in place if appropriate.

> Sometimes I even have found myself dusting the tables or removing broken chairs. We must do whatever is necessary to make the room as comfortable and inviting as possible. The condition of the room that participants enter shapes their very first impression of what is to come.

The way in which educators introduce themselves to participants conveys a message. Individual teachers do have different preferences, depending partly on personality and partly on how they perceive their role.

- Some people choose to greet the students coming in with a welcoming word or two.

- Others like to give students a chance to talk to each other, and so only enter the room when everyone is settled.

- Some plan to enter the room early, but time it so not to be the first person there.

- Some prefer to be in the room before the students but be busy with their preparations.

Where the educator sits or stands also sends a message, suggesting either authority and power or approachability and collegiality.

> It is for this reason that I enter the room with and among the students and sit in the circle, carefully selecting a position that cannot be interpreted as the front of the room. I don't sit, for example, nearest the blackboard. I sit next to someone already present and chat with one or two people while others come in. I feel that I have succeeded when people are surprised to find out that I am the teacher. I have not presented myself as the person who will have the sole power over the coming events. I am a quiet and soft-spoken person, so this way of entering the teaching setting comes naturally to me. It may not work for others. The main point is to avoid shouting, figuratively, "I am the teacher, and you had better prepare yourself to listen to me."

Introducing the Session

Before doing anything else, it is important to establish a comfortable and convivial atmosphere in which participants feel welcome and relaxed.

- Address people by name as soon as possible.

- Prepare nametags in advance if possible and ask participants to put them on as they enter the room.

- Alternatively, bring in 5 x 8 inch index cards and a few felt markers. Have learners fold the cards in half, write their names on them, and prop them up, facing the group, on their tables or desks.

- Use individuals' names as often as possible.

> Recognizing people by name helps us learn their names quickly and makes them feel included by being addressed personally.

The introduction to a course, workshop., or training session is where participants will first see the extent to which the learning experience promises to be interesting and relevant to them. In many adult education contexts, students chose to come based on a course description, workshop flyer, or other publicity. Experienced students may not trust such advertisement, and all

> The first item on the agendas I use is an introductory activity in which participants have an opportunity to talk to each other and get to know something about each other. Doing this immediately establishes the importance of discussion and group development, and creates a comfortable and fun atmosphere. I like to see my classroom buzzing with noise within five minutes of the start time. However, my own teaching is about teaching itself in the context of adult education programs. My students are adult educators or aspiring adult educators. In other contexts, a warm-up activity is probably better placed after the introduction to the content. Therefore, I discuss this in more detail in the next section.

students need to be reassured that will benefit from what is to come.

- Present an agenda or some posting of the order of events for the class or day.

> This provides structure and organization and allows everyone to see what will be happening next at any point in the session.

- Formats may include a simple paper agenda, a PowerPoint presentation, an overhead transparency, or some points on a flip chart or whiteboard.

> In online courses or other distance formats, the presentation of agendas will vary.

- If the content of the course is fixed, that is, if participants have no input in the topics to be covered, this is the time to hand out a schedule of topics.

- Avoid lengthy course outlines of 5 to 10 pages; these are overwhelming for students.

> If necessary, hand out such a document at the end of the first class when people can take it home where they can absorb the content.

- In a one-day workshop, a long outline is unnecessary, but if unavoidable for some reason, circulate it at lunchtime or at least later in the day.

> During the introduction, a concise, clear list of topics and/or objectives is more helpful.

Throughout this impressionable opening session, students are not only interested in content, but also curious about the nature of the upcoming experience. What is the teacher like? Will there be group work? How much will they be expected to read? Are there mandatory assignments? To answer these concerns, the following are suggested.

- Hand out a short statement describing the overall approach of the upcoming sessions, the methods to be used, and information about underlying assumptions, individual and group responsibilities, and necessary constraints.

- Avoid reading to participants, an approach that may seem condescending. Instead, after giving people time to read through the information, ask for comments and questions.

- If participants are to be involved in the selection of topics, the handouts will not include the list of topics or objectives.

> That students will have the opportunity of selecting topics should be included in the overview of approaches, responsibilities, and assumptions. Sometimes, especially when the content is new to people, while initial topics are predetermined, participants select later topics. This, too, needs to be clear right away.

In summary, the three equally important aspects of opening the first session are:

- Be clear about what is to come.

- Ensure that students are interested and find the content and process relevant.

- Ease any discomfort or anxiety that students may feel.

Revealing Values and Showing Respect

In adult education, we often work with participants who are apprehensive about returning to a classroom or people who have not been involved in a learning experience for several years. Even experienced students in a new course will be nervous about who their new classmates are, what the teacher is like, or how difficult the session will be. Many students, for a variety of reasons, have doubts about their ability to learn, read at an appropriate level, make meaningful contributions to discussions, complete learning projects or write papers, and manage their time, given a myriad of other personal and professional commitments. It is because of this common initial anxiety that I do not like to open with a lengthy and potentially intimidating outline or schedule of events. Instead:

- Reassure people that they can do it, that they will succeed and may enjoy the process.

    > Our first goal as educators is to welcome people to the learning experience and enable them to feel more comfortable. While it is usually impossible to achieve this goal immediately as doubts and fears do linger, we must work toward this end.

- Demonstrate to participants that their concerns are shared.

    > For example, make it clear that other members of the group have also been away from studying for a time or have equally pressing family or work responsibilities. Nothing is quite so helpful for increasing comfort as hearing someone say, "I feel that way too."

- Offer reassurance through our own attitudes, values, and style as educators.

    > We must be human, authentic, friendly, and supportive. We need to find a way to relate individually and personally to as many students as quickly as we can. We need to demonstrate our trust in

Apps (1996) writes about "teaching from the heart," bringing our own natural way of caring for others into our teaching. Most adult educators have chosen to enter their profession because of a desire to help others learn or to help others make changes in their lives. If we keep this purpose in mind alongside our basic human respect for others, it will be apparent to our students.

and respect for the abilities and experiences of the people with whom we will be working.

Breaking the Ice

To encourage participants to learn something about each other and share expectations, fears, and something of their lives, a good introductory activity is important. I understand objections to complex or contrived "warm ups" and "ice breakers," which are often forced and embarrassing. I myself do not especially want to hop around like a rabbit, hum a tune, or wear a nametag that says "Patient Patricia." Some people like such activities, and in some contexts, they may work, but I prefer simpler ways of getting people talking to each other.

- Have people introduce themselves in turn to the group and state briefly something about their interests or their professional or personal lives.

    This is the simplest method of breaking the ice. When the participants are experienced and confident and the group is not too large, ordinary introductions can be very effective.

- Remember however that some students often feel quite anxious about having to speak to an unknown group, becoming increasingly nervous as their turn to speak approaches.

> Also probably many people do not remember what was said under these circumstances.

- Get people up out of their chairs, circulating around the room, and talking to each other without putting anyone in the spotlight.

> Books of icebreakers are one source of helpful suggestions for introductory activities.

Here are two easy activities that I have used extensively, either of which may be adapted to a variety of contexts.

Trading Statements

In advance of the session, prepare list of statements, twice as many statements as the number of participants. These can be related to the specific content of the session, be very general, or be a mixture of both. For example, some might read: "I am a grandmother." "I like to sail." "I have more than one pet." "This is the first course [workshop] I've taken in more than six months." "I have read a book on adult education [or any content] in the last year." "I am nervous meeting new people." "I prefer to read a good book rather than go to a movie." "I could be a hermit living in the woods." "I am interested in politics." Write the statements on separate strips of paper or index cards. Give each person two statements at random. Ask people first to read their statements and decide if they describe themselves. They then circulate around the room and trade statements with others in order to collect the statements that best suit them. During this process, participants inevitably exchange information with each other, chat about other matters, and generally begin to relax. This activity lasts no more than ten or fifteen minutes. At the conclusion, an option is to ask if any statements were not traded. When these are read aloud, ask if there is anyone in the room who fits each statement.

Flash Cards

When I was looking for an introductory activity more clearly related to the content of a course but still serving the same purpose of encouraging students to get to know something about each other, I remembered those frightening flash cards from elementary school—the ones with addition or subtraction questions on them that the teacher held up for the class to respond in unison with the answer. In my version, I prepare questions related to the content, as many questions as there are participants. For an introductory course on research methods, these might include, "Are control groups ethical?" "What is an experiment?" "Can teachers do research in their classrooms?" "What does correlation mean?" "Why should research subjects be fully informed about the purpose of the research?" "What is the difference between qualitative and quantitative research?" The questions should not be too difficult, and it does not matter if everyone or even anyone can answer them. Each question is put on an index card, and each person receives one card. People circulate around the room and find as many people as they can who have an answer to the question. They write those names on the back of the card. During these conversations, participants talk about their professions, their experience with the content, and usually other things unrelated to the questions.

At the end of the activity, I may ask if any questions went unanswered. Students often ask if they will know these things by the end of the course, and I assure them that they will. With good questions, interest in the content is stimulated, and I get a sense of the levels of expertise in the group.

Summary

The beginning of any teaching and learning experience creates a first impression that lingers and sets the tone for what is to come. During this crucial time, two equally valuable goals must be met. The first is to clarify what is going to happen and in doing so to connect with learners' interests and needs. The second is to ease students' natural doubts and anxieties, to make them feel comfortable and respected. If either of these goals is ignored, the session that follows will suffer.

In this chapter, I have presented the opening aspects we need to pay attention to, more or less in the order in which they occur. Ensuring that the room is as pleasant as possible and setting it up in a way that encourages equality and interaction among the participants serves to make people comfortable. Introducing the session with a short, clear list of topics and an overview of the planned strategies tells learners what to expect. Showing respect for everyone in the group and including an activity to stimulate conversation among participants adds to people's feeling of comfort.

Chapter Two

Setting the Climate

Farmers and fishermen know a lot about climate. From their point of view it is composed of all of the conditions and circumstances that affect growth and development. In a learning environment, when we consider climate, we are thinking of the atmosphere or mood in the room, including the values and attitudes of participants and teacher. In any gathering of people, large or small, a prevailing mood or tone exists, even though every individual in that group may not share the mood. Following September 11, 2001, the climate in airports was one of fear and distrust; in New York City several months after September 11, the climate had become one of patriotism and caring for others, a reaction to the initial feelings of terror.

Every class has a climate, whether we actively create it or not. The climate of a classroom or workshop setting has a profound impact on the nature of the learning. Students who do their assignments out of fear of punishment or ridicule have a very different learning experience from those who complete learning projects with interest and enthusiasm. People who participate in a discussion because they are genuinely interested in what others have to say on a topic are learning in a very different way from those who talk because they get points for participation. The end product may look the same, but the learning is of a different quality.

Given that a climate develops in every learning group, it is better to deliberately foster the kind of climate we want rather than leave this to chance. In this chapter, I first discuss how we decide on an appropriate climate for our specific teaching situation. I then review five different class climates: challenging, supportive, performing, collaborative, and reflective. I provide suggestions on how to foster each one.

What Kind of Climate Do I Want?

In most adult education texts, only one type of climate is advocated, the one that is supportive and collaborative, in which people are encouraged to gradually assume responsibility for their learning. Consequently, we often hear jokes based on the inappropriateness of this particular teaching and learning climate to what is being taught. For example, we do not want to fly in a plane piloted by those who learned to get in touch with their inner child rather than to read instruments. We do not want a surgeon who had the choice of whether or not to learn anatomy in a self-directed environment. Different disciplines, technical fields, and trades are best learned under certain conditions and circumstances and with certain prevailing attitudes and values, in other words, in certain climates. The first question we need to ask ourselves is: In which climate is my subject most likely to be learned well?

Content is not the only consideration. Additional relevant factors are the characteristics of the participants and the preferences and personality of the educator. A group of mature students reentering a school setting after several years away benefits more from a supportive environment than do a group of managers involved in a leadership seminar. A clerical staff preparing for the implementation of a new and anxiety-provoking technology in the workplace needs a different learning climate than does a group of experienced nurses upgrading a specific skill. This is not to say, as mentioned earlier, that every person in the group will display the same response, but a group mood generally does develop and prevail. We need to ask ourselves, and, in some circumstances our learners, what the most helpful learning climate will be for this particular group. If the answer to this question is not the same answer we get when we consider the requirements of the subject, we usually need to start with the learner group preference and then move over time to what is called for by the content goals.

Finally, we need to consider our own personality, preferences, and style. It is important for an educator to be authentic, that is, to value herself as well as her students, and to present her genuine self in the teaching environment. Good teaching depends on good communication, and we do not communicate well when we are inauthentic. For example, someone who is genuinely caring, supportive, and empathic will find it hard to work in an intensely challenging climate. It is equally difficult for a teacher who has a gift for critical analysis and a naturally penetrating wit to work in an environment where supportiveness is valued over challenge. It is best if we choose areas of practice where our personal strengths and preferences match the needs of the group and the subject.

The Challenging Climate

A challenging climate is one in which participants and facilitator closely examine what they read and see, expect others to justify their opinions, question the authority of an author or other experts, and generally critically analyze their own thoughts and assumptions. A challenging climate is appropriate when the subject is one in which critical thinking is emphasized, the students are experienced and confident, and the educator is comfortable with analyzing and questioning.

The first and perhaps most important thing we can do to establish a challenging climate is to model challenging behavior ourselves in the following ways.

- Present and then question our own point of view on an issue raised in class.

- Argue alternatively for two opposing points of view, making our own thinking process explicit.

- Describe how we developed our current position on a question of interest.

In addition, we must be careful in how we challenge.

- Avoid being too aggressive or argumentative, thereby intimidating students.

     Watch carefully for the students' responses and above all be reasoned and open about what is happening.

- Never simply attack any student's thoughts, ideas, statements, or stories.

  Attack implies weakness versus strength and wrong versus right.

     Good questioning instead seeks to clarify ideas and deepen understanding. Rather than strongly attacking a student's point of view without explanation or warning, make clear that demonstrating the importance of questioning each point of view and analyzing all conclusions is part of the class.

  Soon students will come to see challenge as the norm in the classroom. Once this is established, encourage students to question each other and analyze closely whatever they read, hear, and see.

- When one person presents his opinion, ask who has a different opinion and encourage each participant to elaborate on his or her reasons for that opinion.

     While initially students may find this challenge novel and therefore difficult, they will begin to develop the ability to reason more effectively. Support all attempts to grapple with this process, reinforcing good argument.

- When someone agrees with a statement from a reading or an opinion from the media, ask again who might disagree.

     If no one does, present an opposing viewpoint and ask whether that viewpoint is justified. (In Chapters 16 and 18, I provide examples of activities designed to further this kind of thinking.)

From the outset, work to establish a climate in which everyone is comfortable questioning the authority of a text, the statements of an expert, or the opinions of a classmate. Students will then come to expect and enjoy this intellectual challenge as part of the classroom routine.

To take this one step further, the climate of challenge is one in which participants regularly examine the underlying assumptions they themselves hold. We often base our beliefs on premises of which we are not aware. If someone states, for example, that a nurse must always check and re-check a physician's orders before administering a medication, on what premise is that statement based? That the doctor always knows better than the nurse what a patient requires? That a nurse cannot or should not make a decision herself? Whether we eventually accept or reject these assumptions, they can be questioned. The simplest way of encouraging learners to examine assumptions is to ask "Why?" "Why do you say that?" "Why do you believe that?" "Why do you think that is so?" In a challenging climate, "why?" is a very common question.

The Supportive Climate

A supportive climate is one in which people are helpful, diplomatic, and tactful in assisting each other with the learning. In it, individuals feel cared for, respected, and validated. The supportive climate is appropriate when the subject is threatening, intimidating, or especially difficult. Support is particularly important when learners are anxious, are new to the learning environment, or have fears and doubts about themselves and the learning experience. The educator who is good at creating a supportive climate is one who is empathic, caring, and sensitive to the personal needs and reactions of students. As is the case in establishing any classroom climate, modeling such behavior will quickly set up a group norm. There are many simple but effective ways to set up such norms.

- Use people's names when speaking to them and make regular eye contact with each individual to help participants feel that they are valued members of the group.

    Ideally, each person should experience frequent connection with the educator or someone else in the group; this can be as simple as a look and a smile. (In Chapter 16, I elaborate on some of these strategies.)

- Encourage conversation in small groups or pairs at the very beginning of a session to give students a chance to talk and exchange information without feeling under an uncomfortable spotlight.

    To establish a supportive climate, such small group activities should be easy-going and open-ended. For example, ask students to talk with three or four others about their experiences related to a specific issue under discussion.

- Have each individual meet with a partner and relate an incident from his or her own life.

- Emphasize that people are expected to listen to each other without judgment or questioning.

> In the beginning stages of building a supportive environment, acceptance is essential. As educators, we need to do the same—accept and respect what others say.

- Share our own experiences, especially humorous anecdotes or personal information about ourselves, as a way of encouraging others to participate.

The goal is not only to model the process, but also to present us as ordinary human beings to the class. Students who need support do not need a frightening authority figure as a teacher. For example, when I am working with a group of tradespeople learning how to be teachers, I may mention that my son is a welder and my brother a mechanic. Or, with a group of students returning to school, I may find a time to say how terrified I was to go to university in the big city after growing up in a remote rural community. In order to be authentic such anecdotes must be true, of course, and arise as a natural part of the conversation.

The Performing Climate

A performing climate is one in which the emphasis is placed on carrying out the functions and meeting the requirements of the job. The goal of both participants and educator is the efficient attainment of skills and competencies. The performing climate is appropriate when the goal of teaching or training is that participants become highly skilled in a technical or skills-based subject. It is relevant in the trades, technologies, military, and some professional training and in-service programs. In ideal circumstances, participants are confident and keen to acquire the skills. (If not, combine elements of the supportive climate with the performing climate.) Most often, the educator has experience and expertise with the skills involved.

To establish a performing climate, students should be actually doing things as soon as possible. In some programs, extensive information or theory is presented before students have the opportunity to practice the skills involved. Although there may, in some cases, be a good rationale for this separation of theory and application, the learning process is disrupted as a result. Knowledge does not necessarily transfer easily from a verbal presentation or drawings in a text to practical application, especially when theoretical information is presented several days or even weeks before students can operate the machinery. Thus, to set a climate for performing, include hands-on learning from the beginning and integrate the more abstract concepts as the learning proceeds.

- Send participants into the actual setting—field, lab, shop, sawmill, or hospital—as soon as possible.

    > Even if initially they are only able to observe others or help in small ways, being a part of the action of the physical plant goes a long way towards setting the mood for performance. Students can see what they will learn to do. They can interact with others who have the skills and become familiar with the circumstances in which they will be working.

- Do the same for those who are upgrading skills in the workplace or taking training programs in the field.

Although these people are already part of and familiar with the work setting, it is usually better to teach there than to whisk people off to a conference room or retreat when skill performance is the learning goal.

- Provide many and varied opportunities for doing, practice (repeated doing), and feedback, essential components of the performing climate.

- Have participants work in pairs or small groups, giving each other feedback or simply helping each other with the tasks.

- Make it clear from the outset that each individual will have the chance to perfect the necessary skills.

This does not mean that other facets of learning, such as teamwork and communication, are neglected, but the atmosphere is one in which performing above all is valued. In a sense, the teacher becomes the coach. The environment is one in which everyone works toward the highest level of functioning of all.

When learning skills, mastery or competence must be the goal. Of course, students should also be encouraged to question what they are learning and to propose alternative ways of doing things—they are also learning how to learn. In the end, however, people must master the skills needed to do the job. Thus, the focus is placed on the end product rather than on the process, and this requires a decidedly different climate for learning.

The Collaborative Climate

A collaborative climate is one in which people share their knowledge to generate new ways of seeing and doing things. The collaborative climate is appropriate when we want students to learn to work together to create new understandings by sharing their experiences and expertise. The subject must be one in which there are no definitive answers or solutions so that people can pool their knowledge to develop new ways of viewing problems or issues. Any discipline involving social issues or working with people falls into this category. In the ideal collaborative environment, participants have experience with the subject, enjoy working with others, and are confident of their abilities. If this is not the case, aspects of the supportive climate may need to be part of their learning experience. The educator should have strong interpersonal skills and view the subject in a constructivist fashion. He should prefer working with people as opposed to "getting the task done."

In order to build this climate actively involve participants right from the beginning through all manner of interactive strategies—discussion, group work, role plays, debates, case studies.

- Design discussions and activities that have no definite or "correct" answers.

- Pose open-ended questions with a variety of possible outcomes.

- Encourage participants to offer their own experiences and knowledge.

> A general suggestion to "tell us your experience with this issue," or "recall your best (or worst) experience with this problem" can cultivate this style of interaction. For example, in a communications course for hospitality industry workers, who are trying to create guidelines for dealing with upset customers, participants can be asked to recall and describe a difficult interaction they had with a customer at the

front desk. Relating this experience to the group encourages others to bring their own resources to the collaborative work.

- To set the climate, we must model the collaborative style.

  Contribute to the collaboration just as participants are expected to do, that is, relate and apply experience and expertise to the problem but do not attempt to determine the direction of the process.

- Never indicate, directly or indirectly, that specific responses or answers are expected.

  Nothing shuts down a collaborative climate faster than an educator who manipulates discussion in the direction of a predetermined end, or even worse, waits until people construct a response and then gives his interpretation. Given the intrinsic power of the position of a teacher, students assume the teacher's interpretation is correct. Once the collaborative climate is accepted, the educator can give his opinion, which will be merely one of several.

The Reflective Climate

A reflective climate is one in which personal growth and development are the primary goals, and participants must establish their own position on issues. The reflective climate differs from the challenging climate in that participants' questioning and thinking is focused inwardly rather than on ideas presented by others or issues in the larger world. When we talk about a "reflective practitioner," for example, we are talking about a person who thinks about what she does, who questions her performance or values or assumptions, with the goal of improving her practice. A workshop for practicing teachers may call for a reflective climate. Learners should have a fair amount of knowledge and experience with the subject. A reflective climate is not appropriate when people are learning skills for the first time. In that case, while reflection should still be encouraged, it should not be the primary characteristic of the learning climate. In order to be reflective, learners also need some degree of self-awareness and a willingness to be open about mistakes or weaknesses. Likewise, the educator needs to be self-aware, willing to share her own reflections, and comfortable taking risks.

To encourage a reflective climate the following suggestion may be helpful.

- We should incorporate time for reflection into the learning experience.

  > I often start a workshop for practicing educators or health professionals with a "quiet time" for thought about a topic. Over the course of the day, I also include two or three quiet times for reflection. Initially, as this is not a usual practice, participants may be startled, but a reflective climate begins to grow.

- Journals can be used to foster reflection.

  > Ask participants to keep journals starting with the first session. In a one-day workshop, unfortunately, the technique is not practical, unless time is allotted during the day for journal entries.

  > Reflective journals tend to work best if few or no guidelines are given. People should write what they want in a style that is comfortable for them.

  > Dialogue journals, in which learners exchange journals with a classmate and write back and forth to each other, are very effective.

- We should always respond to reflective journals by sharing our reactions to what is written.

  > It is important for students to receive recognition of such personal effort. (See Chapter 19 on giving feedback.)

- If journals are too time-consuming or inappropriate for other reasons, we can ask students to provide quick reflections at the end of each session or part way through full-day sessions.

  > I call this a "Quick Check." I give students a 3 x 5 inch index card and ask them to note on one side of the card what has been positive for them in their learning experience and on the other side what they would prefer to be different. They can choose to make their comments anonymously or not, as they wish. I transcribe their responses and return them to the group for discussion and further reflection. This technique also serves to get feedback from learners as I discuss in Chapter 11.

- The educator needs to demonstrate that she is reflective. This can be accomplished by talking about personal reflections as a matter of course. I keep a reflective teaching journal for each course that I facilitate, and recently, I experimented sharing excerpts from my teaching journal with the students as a way of modeling reflection. I handed out one page of my reflections at the beginning of each class, using that as a review of the previous class and a stimulus for discussion, as well as a model of reflection. Modeling is important here as in any learning climate.

Summary

An atmosphere prevails in any teaching and learning setting whether or not we deliberately create it. I suggest that it is better to determine what kind of atmosphere is appropriate for the subject, the learners, and us, and set out to establish it. In this chapter, I discuss five different climates and provide some ideas for setting up and fostering each. However, as things are never so clear-cut in practice as in theory, the appropriate climate may be some combination of the five presented or even something quite different. With practice, we learn to mix and match the various facets of the classroom atmospheres to suit the situation or even the moment. It is also important to remember that individual learners have different styles and preferences, which may not fit the chosen climate.

The challenging climate is one in which the participants question what they read and see, and critically examine the ideas presented. The supportive climate is one in which people are caring and helpful in assisting each other with learning. The performing climate is one in which people are concerned with the efficient attainment of skills and competencies. The collaborative climate is one in which people pool their experiences and knowledge to generate new knowledge. The reflective climate is one in which people are encouraged to focus on their own thoughts and ideas with the goal of personal development and growth. As educators, our responsibility is to create a mosaic from these climates, one that fluctuates with and responds to the changing needs of the group.

Chapter Three

Creating Opportunities for Learners to Have a Say

Recently, I gave a one-hour workshop for university teachers from a variety of disciplines—biology, chemistry, social work, nursing, library science, business, education. The topic was how to turn your insights about teaching into published works. It was a tall order for one hour. I prepared an overview of the kinds of articles people could write, composed lists of journals open to publishing such work, and included a collection of conferences on teaching and learning where people could submit proposals for presentations. As we went around the room introducing ourselves, I realized that every person had come to this hour with individual expectations of what he or she would learn. Perhaps my ideas of what should be included in this hour had nothing to do with who they were and what they hoped for. I abandoned my planned agenda and asked people to talk about what they had written, what they hoped to write, what problems they had encountered, and generally, why they came. Some wanted to talk about how to make that leap from an idea in one's head to words on paper. Some wanted to know how to find the time to write and stay motivated. Some did not have specific expectations but were just generally interested in the idea of writing about teaching. One science professor said he had never thought about this possibility before he read the advertisement for the workshop.

I had not believed it possible in only one hour to devise any practical way for participants to have input into the content of the workshop. And I did not think this possible even after decades of telling others that learners should always have a say in their learning experience. I did give out my lists and talked for a few minutes about the kinds of articles people could write, but we spent most of the hour exchanging ideas about the questions that individuals raised. There was applause at the end, and the participants said they felt inspired.

People have a much greater commitment to learning and change when they are involved in deciding what is going to happen. Whatever we teach and whatever our constraints, it is essential to incorporate participants' needs, interests, and goals into the learning experience. This principle should be put into practice as soon as possible. There is little point in handing out a full course outline and then asking people what they want to learn, or worse, asking people what they want to learn and *then* handing out the full course outline. In this chapter, I discuss some approaches to involving learners in decision-making about their learning.

Selecting Topics

The most basic decision we make about the learning experience is what is to be learned. Most teachers immediately object to students choosing content for one of several reasons. First, they argue the students are simply not familiar enough with the subject area—they do not even know what they need to know. Further, a well-established curriculum must be followed in order to cover the necessary course material. As well, basic essential skills or competencies must be learned in order to meet academic, trade, or professional requirements. Last, many students attend courses and workshops in order to earn a credit or because they are required to come. Of course, these arguments have validity.

However, on the other hand, I have met educators who work in these circumstances and have managed to incorporate students' ideas into the selection of topics. For example, I recently interviewed a teacher of introductory 18th century literature, a subject about which his students know next to nothing at the beginning of the course. He sends them off to the library at the first class to look at a variety of texts on 18th century literature and bring back questions they gather. These questions are divided into various types, some of them becoming projects on which the students work in groups over the term. The students are entirely responsible for selecting the topics within the limits of the content as found in appropriate texts.

I lead a course on research methods, another area where the learners have no experience or expertise. After an overview of the basic research paradigms, students work in groups to generate topics they want to explore.

Often curriculum is not as predetermined as we think it is. In addition, students often select topics that we would include ourselves, but they have made the decision and therefore feel responsible, involved, and listened to. Here are some suggestions to give learners the opportunity to have a say in the topics of a workshop or course.

- Before a workshop begins, ask participants what they would like to discuss.

- When students have some expertise or experience with the subject, ask them to work in groups to decide on the topics to be studied.

  > This process can be completely open-ended or students can work from a given list or the tables of content of pre-selected books.

- Set the required topics, those that must be covered for whatever reason, and ask students to choose the remaining topics.

- When students simply do not know what they want to learn or have come because they have to, ask indirectly.

  > Ask about their experiences, concerns, and lives; then help them make connections to the content that they cannot yet see themselves.

- Provide the necessary basic information, then ask students to branch out in directions of their choosing.

  > Even if the only time available for student choice is one or two classes or one hour of a workshop, use it to work with topics participants select during that time.

Selecting Strategies

It is easy enough to fall into a rut and repeatedly use the same teaching methods. We often confuse familiar teaching with effective teaching; if our techniques are comfortable for us, we tend to believe they must be so for others and therefore work well. I recall one very candid group who finally said to me, "Can we just *not* do group work for a little while?" It is important for learners to have some say about the methods by which they are instructed. As experienced educators, we know which method works well with a particular subject or topic, but usually several strategies will work just as well with that particular subject or topic, leaving us able to respond to our students' preferences. Students' motivation increases when they are able to make decisions about their learning. Perhaps just as importantly, students generally know how they best learn—we need to learn that from them.

Giving students a voice in the selection of the learning strategies can be accomplished formally or informally, regularly or spontaneously.

- Formally, have students gather in pairs or groups (or individually, though this is more cumbersome). Working from a list of either self-generated or given topics, ask them to suggest what they think would be an ideal way to learn about these topics. After compiling the suggestions, the group must arrive at a consensus on the preferred method.

  > This process usually works very well. People are generally interested in the ideas of others and open to trying a variety of approaches. If consensus does not

exist, it may be possible to divide a group into two or three subgroups where each learns in its preferred way.

To see the strategies students propose is fascinating; they often have new ideas that we educators have not used. In addition, they sometimes are familiar with relevant resources—videos, books, articles, —and suggest incorporating these into the learning experience. I frequently have students offer to lead an activity or bring in a colleague who is an expert in an area. In this way, an exciting variety of learning strategies can be created.

- On a more informal level, a moment arrives in any session when things are just not going well. This is the ideal time to stop and say; "This isn't working. What should we do instead?"

- Students appreciate us noticing and asking their opinion, and inevitably will have a good suggestion. However, we do not need to wait until the session or class is derailed. When appropriate, it is easy to say, "We could do this in groups or in a large group discussion; which would you prefer?" Or, "Next week, we're going to be talking about how to close a sales call. Would you rather watch a video or read this article?" The Quick Check (see Chapter 2) is also an excellent source of information about students' preferences for different learning strategies.

When they tell us what they enjoy and what they would like to see changed, we need to act on what they say.

Bringing in Resources

When asked to contribute ideas about learning strategies, students often suggest resources. Adult learners have diverse interests and experiences to call on; they usually have chosen to attend a course or workshop because it matches an interest or fulfills a need. As educators of adults, we must not think of ourselves as the only ones who know the subject. When given the opportunity, students will bring in an intriguing array of resources to the classroom.

Some teachers deliberately ask participants to select a topic for which they will be responsible for finding materials to present to the group. Although this can work well, some individuals may end up with topics for which they have no special enthusiasm. I find it better to make this process open-ended, that is, encourage students to bring resources in, but neither require them to do so nor assign specific topics. Some people may never contribute anything, but that need not be a concern. The aim is to get the norm established—that the group values all contributions of materials.

> If my students neither bring in resources nor offer to do so spontaneously, I may privately ask a student whom I know has expertise if he or she can think of anything to bring to a particular discussion. Once it starts, it snowballs. Everyone likes to contribute a favorite reading, poem, or newspaper clipping. People come with videos or bring in their laptop computers to show others a website they have discovered. In online courses, I find students are especially generous in sharing website links.

Leading Sessions

Many educators, for a variety of reasons or simply because of tradition, expect or require students to give presentations. Sometimes, there is a good rationale for this. For example, if students are learning to be teachers, it is helpful for them to practice teaching with their peers. However, in some situations, I find no good reason to insist on student presentations, although I do encourage learners to facilitate a session or part-session as a way of having a voice in the learning experience. Here are some ways to encourage active student involvement in learning sessions.

- Tell students early in the course that any time they want to try out an activity or share their expertise with others in the group this can be accommodated in the schedule.

    Just as in establishing the practice of bringing in resources, this too has to start somewhere.

- Ask people privately if they would like to lead a session or make a presentation, but first make sure that they will not interpret this request as a requirement.

    Again, once student leaders or presenters emerge, they continue to do so. People may not volunteer to lead a session until nearer the end of a course when they are more comfortable or excited about what they are learning, but the opportunity should be available from the beginning.

In one of my courses, *Adult Learning in the Workplace*, shortly after we had sat down, one of the participants said with considerable enthusiasm, "Could I just present something to the group? Something I'm trying to understand? I need some feedback." We abandoned our usual opening, and the student went straight to the blackboard to present the ideas with which she was struggling. Although this happened spontaneously, I do not think it would have occurred had it not been clear that we valued individual contributions.

In a short workshop, individual involvement in the learning experience is much less practical and less likely to occur. Nevertheless, it is still possible, although contributions will have to be shorter.

- When someone does indicate he or she has something to contribute, we should give up our own agenda to allow this to happen.

   For example, a participant may say something that reveals he has the experience or some expertise that would be of benefit to the entire group. We can then ask for more. In workshops I have facilitated a participant has often raced out of the room to collect something from his office to present to the group.

Choosing Learning Projects

> Learning projects are assignments, papers, or projects of any kind that students engage in to further or demonstrate their learning (see Chapter Fifteen). Where grades or credits are given, learning projects usually are included as part of the evaluation process. In non-credit or more informal educational experiences, learners may participate in projects in order to advance their knowledge, apply what they are learning, or simply experiment with new ideas or skills. Students should almost always have some say in choosing their learning projects.

- The ideal is for students to be allowed to choose among different options to demonstrate learning.

    Of course, essential competencies must be demonstrated for licensing or certification, and when fundamental skills or knowledge are required. However, I have seen trades teachers, who have long lists of necessary skills for their students to master, develop very creative alternatives for students to display their accomplishments.

- In some circumstances, the choice of learning projects can be completely open-ended.

    I have seen paintings, poetry, photography, sculptures, quilts, autobiographies, short stories, and videos, alongside the regular essays and presentations. Recent favorites include a metal sculpture constructed by a welding instructor depicting how his classroom would appear and a quilt made by a returning graduate student showing her personal development story.

- In other circumstances, educators may provide students with a list of options and topics.

> It is best if students can have a choice in both the format and the content of their learning projects, that is, in selecting a written or a verbal presentation, as well as the topic itself. However, if writing or presentation skills or both are essential skills in themselves, then giving people control over the topics may be the best we can do. I would encourage educators to make every effort to do this, as the learning is more meaningful for students. They can bring in their interests and experience. They can take their preferred learning style into consideration. They will feel a much stronger commitment to the work.

- Students also can have a say in when their projects are due.

> I recently interviewed a botany teacher who asks her students to make up a schedule of when they will complete each assignment in the course. Each individual student has a separate set of deadlines. The teacher gives everyone two coupons that they can use when they cannot meet their deadlines; if they do not use the coupons, they receive a few extra points. This system is difficult to keep track of, but well worth the effort to help students learn how to take charge of their learning.

Summary

I often think of other aspects of life when I think through how best to facilitate learning. Although education has become institutionalized—placed in classroom settings and divided into specific blocks of time—learning is really a part of everyday life. If someone tells us, "You have to take out the garbage every Tuesday night by 6:00 p.m.," it is quite different from asking, "Of these chores we need to do, which will you do?" At work, an autocratic boss is far less likely to gain our commitment to the job than is one who involves us in making decisions about what needs to be done. Learning is no different. People are involved when they have a voice—in what they are going to learn, in how they will learn it, in what resources they will use, in what learning projects they will engage in, and, in addition, when they have the opportunity to participate in teaching through leading sessions. They care about what happens in the learning environment because they have played a part in shaping it. In this chapter, I offer some ideas on what this means in practice and some suggestions on how to create opportunities for learners to have some control.

The idea that involvement produces commitment cannot be overstated. Human beings have a basic need for freedom to make choices about their own lives. Surely, it is essential that we meet this need in the learning environment.

Chapter Four

Fostering Student Responsibility for Learning

A fisherman from the area where I live in the Maritimes recalls his time in training for his job—learning to set nets, operate the boat, and work with the ropes. His supervisor told him what to do, how to do it, and used punitive feedback, making him feel "only this high" when he made a mistake. He had no responsibility for his learning; he felt powerless. A co-worker eventually took over, working with him rather than over him, and the fisherman-in-training quickly began to pick up the skills he needed and gain confidence in his ability to learn. This time, he felt responsible and wanted to do well.

In Chapter Three, I discuss some ways in which participants can have some say in what goes on in the learning environment. Making decisions about learning is one important way to foster students' responsibility for their own learning, but there are many other small yet meaningful ways in which this can be done. How individual educators encourage students to take responsibility will vary. One day, in a conversation with a friend and colleague, he remarked that I tend to withdraw to the edge of the group whereas he remains actively engaged with the members. Yet we share the same goals in our teaching. We both strive to share the responsibility for learning with our students.

In this chapter, I discuss some ideas and strategies to help people take on a sense of responsibility: being a co-learner, leaving students alone, asking rather than telling, and "each one teach one." I do not give a comprehensive set of suggestions, but trust that those that I do make will lead teachers to take responsibility for finding their own personal strategies.

Being a Co-Learner

Being a co-learner means learning alongside students, learning from them and their experiences, and combining our ideas as educators and our students' ideas to create something new. As Brookfield (1990) points out, we must never pretend ignorance of a subject in which we are expert—students will quickly detect and dislike such inauthentic behavior. Being open to learning with students is revealed and expressed through our attitudes and values. It involves respecting the expertise and experience of students and wanting to know more about them, who they are, what they do, what they know. Rather than assuming that only our own knowledge is valuable because we are teachers, and rather than telling everything we know because we do not think others know much, we are open to and interested in what we can learn from others.

Co-learning, learning together, ensures that everyone is responsible for the learning. One person does not hand out knowledge to another person, like a package, or as in Freire's (1970) banking model in which teachers deposit knowledge into passive students. Instead, people work together, each with different understandings and experiences, to generate knowledge. In disciplines where the knowledge is instrumental in nature, that is, technical or scientific, a large base of concrete information already exists. We do not re-create that information every time we teach. It is factual; it is already there. This is not to say that we cannot find new and innovative ways of seeing or expressing instrumental knowledge. However, to be a true co-learner in this context is probably not possible. Yet I think, for example, of problem-based learning where students work together to discover the facts they need in order to solve larger, integrative problems. For example, students may work to solve a problem on how to divert a stream in a town while leaving the surrounding environment undamaged. To do this, they need to acquire information of various kinds, as well as consider social concerns. In this kind of scenario, the educator easily becomes a co-learner.

When we fragment knowledge by simply giving students a package of facts to take away with them to memorize, the facts have no context and little meaning. Students have no responsibility for the process, other than to accept and absorb the package. When people get responsibly involved in learning, no matter how fixed the content, they learn more effectively. Consequently, they have better access to the information, which has been more fully processed.

Regardless of the subject in which we work, we need to look for ways to learn with the learners and consequently to share the responsibility for the learning process with them.

Leave Students Alone

This curious section heading may startle readers, but I remember how I learned this lesson. Many years ago I organized an event featuring Malcolm Knowles, the renowned adult educator, who came to speak at the university where I worked. The lecture hall was full and buzzing with anticipation. I had escorted Professor Knowles to the podium. The introductions made, I left the room to attend to an organizational matter. Only five or ten minutes after the session had begun, I was startled to see Professor Knowles strolling down the hallway, cigarette in hand. "What's wrong?" I asked. "Oh, they're busy learning," he calmly replied. All three hundred of them? How could this be possible? But Malcolm Knowles knew when to leave people alone to learn.

Leaving students alone implies that the educator trusts them to be involved in learning without supervision or monitoring. This, in turn, leads students to feel responsible. When we monitor others, we create dependence. Students may think that if the teacher is "not looking," they can take advantage to talk about something else. Or, they may come to feel they always need the teacher nearby for support while working. In either case, constant overseeing fosters childlike behavior. I am not suggesting that learners who are having difficulty or want the teacher's help should be ignored, but rather that at times it is best to count on people being able to work on their own.

- When participants are working in groups, it is often appropriate to let them work without intervention.

> A tradition in adult education has arisen in which the facilitator circulates around the room and randomly joins groups or stands nearby looking over the shoulders of group members. I followed that practice for years but became increasingly uncomfortable with it. Sometimes people would stop talking. Alternatively, they would center their attention on me or appear to invent a question to ask me. I began to feel like an intruder in their learning process. When I finally stopped monitoring group work, I not only enjoyed my role more, but also became convinced that the groups were more productive.
>
> I now usually sit and read, remaining available for anyone who wants to bring me into the discussion. Sometimes I disappear entirely. This decision depends on the maturity, experience, and confidence of the participants. In a workshop, where I do not know people well, I always make myself available.

- Obviously, there are times when this strategy is not appropriate.

> For example, if students are working with expensive equipment or when safety is an issue, the teacher should never leave the area.

- Leaving students alone at times during large group discussions is also helpful.

> If the goal of a discussion is that participants are to create new understandings of issues by sharing experiences and opinions, it obviously is best if the

discussion takes place among participants rather than continually being channeled through the facilitator. Again, this seems to be a matter of trust. If we believe that people are capable of constructing knowledge without our intervention, then we need to demonstrate that by giving them the opportunity to do so.

During this process, I am not suggesting that we get up and leave the room, (although on occasion this is advantageous), but instead that we withdraw to the edge of the discussion. I deliberately use eye contact to manage this process, especially in the beginning of the discussion. That is, when a student makes a comment while looking at and therefore speaking to me, I look away. When she finishes speaking, I remain silent and look to others in the group for a response. If none comes, I may nudge the process by asking what others think. It does not take long for people to start talking to each other rather than to the teacher.

- It is important to be consistent in avoiding supervision in order to establish it as a group norm.

The educator's role becomes one of commenting or sharing experiences as another member of the group. He or she may also take responsibility for gently guiding the discussion back on track if it wanders too far off topic and for summarizing what has been said. However, participants can also assume these roles in some cases. People can take turns wrapping up the discussion or noticing when it goes too far afield.

- We need to allow silence to exist in a classroom or workshop; we should not jump into the silent spaces.

Silence gives people time to reflect on what was said and serves to calm the room. It furthers student responsibility for learning primarily because it is a time

when the teacher has withdrawn from the process and
has ceased to control it.

Asking Rather than Telling

When I overhear an educator saying in a loud voice, "Now, I want you
to..." I cringe. Perhaps It reminds me of childhood school days when teachers
commonly directed us to take out our books and turn to page so-and-so or do
problems 7 to 9. If we want people to be responsible, we must curtail the
tendency to tell them what to do. A person who is told what to do is not
responsible but merely following orders.

To advance student responsibility is often a difficult and subtle process of
achieving a balance. As educators, *we* are also responsible. We are responsible
for providing guidance, for knowing our subject, for creating a learning
environment that works, for selecting activities and readings that lead to
learning, and so on. At the same time, we should not assume a position of
control by ordering people around—do this and then do that. Not if we want
them to be responsible for their own learning. Every educator needs to find his
or her own way of handling this, but the general guideline of asking rather
than telling may be helpful. Here are some examples of how to implement
this:.

- We can ask rather than tell participants about practical matters of
  classroom management.

  > For example, we can ask when people would like to
  > take a break and for how long; if they would prefer

that the session starts or finishes at a different time; whether or not they want to bring refreshments to class; or if they would prefer getting the agenda for the session in advance via e-mail.

Initially, questions of this kind sometimes annoy people—they consider it time wasted and are used to being told what to do. However, giving students the opportunity to make these decisions can be part of establishing an environment in which they are responsible.

- Asking participants about the teaching strategies can be helpful.

    "Would you rather do this individually or in small groups or in the large group?" "Would you like to take some time to review this reading before we discuss it?" "Do you have discussion questions you would like us to pay attention to as we address this reading?" "We could develop a role-play related to this issue. Would you be interested in doing that?" Asking these sorts of questions shows that the educator is willing to be flexible in responding to students' choices.

- We should ask rather than tell how much time should be allotted to learning activities.

    In order to manage time, students are often told how much time to spend on an activity: "You have 20 minutes to do this before you report back." I used to do this as well, thinking that it clarified my expectations. However, after being on the receiving end of this kind of direction on several occasions, I realized just how limiting it really is. Just when the group is deeply engaged in an intriguing discussion of one of the points in the activity, someone is blowing a whistle and yelling that we have only one minute left. Nothing destroys a sense of responsibility faster than that.

Now, I say, "We'll see how long it takes" or "Can you let me know how long you think you'll need once you get going?" Students may be uncomfortable at first but soon come to value the freedom to complete the activity in peace. Sometimes one group or, if an individual activity, a few individuals finish ahead of others, but people usually appreciate the chance to relax, read, or take a break while others finish. It takes a bit of practice to adjust the timing of the entire session when the time required for specific activities cannot be predicted, but is well worth the effort.

- We need to give many options as we can and offer students the opportunity to make choices in as many areas as possible.

For example, we can assign two or three readings but ask people to choose the one they will do. If the readings present different perspectives on the same issue, we can ask students who have read one article to summarize it for those who read a different article. Options within learning activities can be provided.

If a role-play or a debate is underway, for example, students should have the option of either playing and debating or being an observer or recorder for the activity. This allows people who are more introverted to opt out of an uncomfortable situation, but most importantly, it puts the responsibility for deciding how to participate on the learner.

Each One Teach One

In one of my courses during the last term, one of the students said, "We're all teachers in this course." In adult education, we are working with people who have a wealth of experience and knowledge, and when they are encouraged to teach their peers what they know, we are truly fostering student responsibility for the learning process. Some basic techniques follow.

- We need to create an environment in which people are free to share their experiences.

    > This is a simple matter of asking: "What are your experiences related to this issue?" "How would you do this in your practice?" "Who has a story about this?" People enjoy talking about their experiences and will do so readily as soon as it is clear that the group and the educator value these contributions.

- We can organize peer teaching—students teaching each other—in a more formal way as well.

    > Students can select topics to investigate in more depth than is possible to do in the larger group (they can work on this in pairs or small groups) and subsequently teach the rest of the class what they have learned.

    > Sometimes this is done through fairly formal presentations, but I prefer to ask people to teach rather than to present information. In other words, they set up a discussion or learning activity rather than lecturing. The key to success in this technique is that students are free to choose topics of particular interest to their professional or personal lives. If our goal is to encourage student responsibility, topics should not be assigned.

Summary

There are some paradoxes inherent in encouraging students to be responsible. We cannot, for example, "make" anyone responsible. Assuming responsibility can only come from within each person. So what we are doing then, as adult educators, is trying to set up an environment where this naturally and inevitably happens. Some of the suggestions I make in this chapter involve walking a fine line between challenging people to taking responsibility and creating a situation in which they will want and choose to do so.

When we become co-learners with our students, we learn from them just as they learn from us. Knowledge is not like money in a cash machine, something that we hand out to people, but rather something that we investigate and create together. When we leave students alone rather than monitor what they do, we trust them to learn, and demonstrate our belief in their ability to do so. When we ask people what they want to do rather than tell them what to do, we place responsibility on their shoulders. When we encourage people to teach each other what they know, we remove ourselves from the role of expert and send the message to our students that we *know* they are responsible for their learning

Chapter Five

Understanding Learning Styles

The theory of learning style, that is, that people have different preferences as to how they best learn, has grown in popularity in the field of adult education over the past three or four decades. Unfortunately, it has grown so much in popularity that we have ended up with people walking around with name tags reading "blue" or "gold" or "INTP" or "ESFJ." A solid understanding of learning style can certainly help us better work with students, but we must take care not to stereotype, label, or allow people to use their learning preferences as a rationale for avoiding specific activities.

Most educators, whether or not they modify their teaching in order to take learning style theory into account, are familiar with the concept. But the most commonly asked question, and rightly so, is just what should we do with this knowledge? Do we have to teach everything several times to appeal to each identified learning style? How can we possibly find the time to do that? Which of many models of learning styles do we follow? Should we encourage students to develop other learning styles or cater to the one they prefer? These are valid and meaningful questions, and the usual answer is that we should provide enough variety in our teaching methods so that something each student prefers is included. But does that not mean that at any given time, the majority of the students are not being engaged? It reminds me of the notion of teaching to the middle of the class, a place where no one actually is.

In this chapter, I first provide an overview of learning style theory; next, I discuss some ways to respond to students' preferences. My understanding of learning style is based on Jung's (1921 [1971]) work on psychological type. Although there are many systems for classifying learning preferences, I find that psychological type theory incorporates most other systems. It is universally appealing, and I have found it to be, in my own practice, the most meaningful interpretation of the differences in how individuals like to learn. When understood as Jung intended, this theory also has the added advantage of not stereotyping people or boxing them into a category from which they never escape. No one should have to wear a nametag that says, "Hi, my name is Cheryl, and I'm a blue."

Learning Style Based on Psychological Type

Some individuals are more focused inwardly and others outwardly. That is, some people are more interested their own perceptions, judgments, and reactions while others are more interested in the things outside of themselves, the things in the world. The inward focus is called introversion and the outer focus extraversion. Every person displays both of these characteristics but in varying degrees, and most people prefer one to the other. When learning, more introverted people like to work with material that has personal meaning, content that they can relate to their own sense of self. They also often prefer to read or work alone, or work in pairs or small groups. Extraverted people, on the other hand, are more outgoing and interested in ideas, issues, values, and perceptions that exist outside of them when they are learning. They would rather talk things through with others than think them through by themselves.

There are also two ways people can make judgments or decisions. When people use the thinking function, they make judgments based on logic and reason. When people use the feeling function, they make judgments based on values, their own and the values of others. When Jung (1921 [1971] uses the word "feeling," he is not referring to emotions as we do in our everyday use of the word. He is writing about a rational process of making judgments based on a desire for harmony with other people. Again, everyone has both of these functions but usually prefers one more than the other. While learning, people who favor the thinking function like things to be organized, structured, and logical. This matches their way of working through problems. People who favor the feeling function are more interested in learning with and through people—getting to know others, working with others, and understanding others' reactions.

Similarly, there are two ways people perceive things around them. When people use the sensing function, they use their five senses to gather information. This means that they are grounded in the present, and concrete reality is perceived through their senses. When people use the intuitive function, they see things through hunches, imagination, and possibility. This means that they are future-oriented and interested in what could be rather than what is. Everyone has some degree of both sensing and intuition but usually tends to use one function more regularly than the other. When learning, people who use the sensing function like things to be realistic and tangible. They learn through doing. More intuitive people are attracted to things that are imaginative, creative, and original. They learn by following a vision.

Everybody has a profile of preferences. That is, they display introversion and extraversion, thinking and feeling, and sensing and intuition, all developed to varying degrees. Some people have quite strong preferences, others not, but each of these characteristics exists in each person.

Learning Style and The Structure of Teaching

By the structure of teaching, I mean the organization or framework within which teaching and learning takes place. Some classes run along like well-oiled machines with everything taking place as expected; these classes are carefully organized and planned, and events follow the plan. Other classes are busy and noisy with people moving from group to group, talking and laughing. Still others are free and open with no visible plan; teacher and learners alike go with what happens. We usually do not consciously decide on a structure of teaching—it comes from our own personality and preferences. But it makes a big difference to the students whose preferences are different from our own.

In a research project I conducted with a colleague, we explored how educators adapt to a new context and how they learn to work together as a team (Cranton and Carusetta, 2001). One theme that emerged was the difference between what we labeled intuitive teaching and planned teaching. Teachers who preferred one style more than the other experienced a great deal of frustration in learning to work together at the beginning of the project. Over the course of the year, they did come to deeply value this difference and rely on each other's strengths. What was at work here was their difficulty in dealing with a structure of teaching that went against their grain, one favored by someone with a strong intuitive function versus one favored by someone with a strong thinking function. Students will have the same experience of frustration if they find themselves in a learning situation where the structure goes against their preference.

One solution is compromise. The teacher who is more comfortable with a carefully planned session that follows an agenda needs to allow some time for going with the flow of ideas or discussion. In relaxing her agenda to some extent, she will come to appreciate the value of doing so—she will learn from her more intuitive students at the same time as she meets their learning needs. The teacher who likes to wing it needs to incorporate a schedule, even if it is loose, so that the students who want to know where they are going have some of that structure. It need not be a constraint. One of my colleagues, who prefers the more intuitive style of teaching, writes his outline for a session on chart paper then feels free to cross off, change, or add items as he goes. His students can easily see the structure of the session, and he feels free to let things evolve.

Learning Style and Teaching Methods

There are two approaches to reconciling teaching methods with learning style. Both are valid.

- The first approach is to try to match teaching methods to learning styles, to use techniques that fit in with the preferences of the participants as much as possible.

  > This involves either finding out what students' styles are by using a learning styles inventory or assuming that all or most styles are present in any one group. Then, we can devise different ways of working with the material to cater to each style.

- Rather than consider participants' preference, another technique is to work toward helping them develop alternative learning styles.

  > The assumption is that when the method used does not match the person's preference, this helps the person to learn to use another style, which is a useful accomplishment.

If both of these approaches are valid, and I think they are, then the dilemma starts to disappear. Whatever method we use helps in some way. It is essential, though, that this be done deliberately and openly. We need to select methods for the various learning preferences consciously and be sure that students are aware of what we are doing and why. If students know that a particular technique will help them learn to learn in a different way, this helps ease frustration.

Students who are more introverted will enjoy some quiet time for reflection and opportunities to work alone. Those who are more extraverted will appreciate activities that allow them to be out in the world doing things and talking with others. People who have a preference for thinking enjoy organization, structure, and logically presented information. Those who prefer feeling relish the opportunity to work in groups and get to know their classmates. Students who use their sensing function want practical and concrete things to do. Those who use intuition would rather create new opportunities and work out ways to reform things. Teaching methods that draw on each of these ways of being can be incorporated in most learning situations.

We can ensure that students understand what methods we are using and why.

- For example, we can point out when a strategy is one that intuitive learners will particularly enjoy. The comment, "You must know someone who learns this way," or a question such as, "How does that feel to you?" helps students focus on the match between the method and the learning preference.

- If group work is a regular part of the teaching and learning environment, we could consider learning styles in the composition of the groups.

> It can be a great pleasure for people to work with others who share their preferences; this can also be very insightful for people who are coming to understand their learning style. Like-style groups have their weaknesses though and should not be used exclusively. It is equally important for people to see others' strengths and learn how a mixed group can work together.

Learning Styles and Learning Materials

In education, we tend to rely on the printed word as our primary learning material. Even in practical fields such as the trades, what is called "theory" is often separated from practice, and students study from textbooks in the classroom before applying what they have learned in the shop or field. We not only rely on print materials, but also certain kinds of print materials—books and articles that present things in an intellectual, logical, rational fashion. There is a long tradition of associating intelligence and success in school with the use of the psychological preference for the thinking function. The system perpetuates itself as those who become teachers are usually those who were themselves successful in school and therefore successful in using printed materials to learn.

Recently, in the adult education literature, some writers have been promoting the importance of nurturing creativity and imagination (Dirkx, 2000), discussing the role of emotion in learning (Wiessner and Mezirow,

2001), and exploring how the body learns (Michelson, 1998). In addition, experiential learning, or learning by doing, has been with us for decades and has been foundational in shaping adult education. These forays into facets of learning other than the cognitive and rational are important and need to be considered in relation to learning styles and the materials we use to foster learning.

- People who prefer the thinking function learn well from the typical rational presentation of material through books and articles.

- Those who tend to use their feeling function may prefer to learn from people–from being with others, hearing their stories, and simply working together.

  > I assume that they also learn well from videos or movies, especially those that focus on the human element.

- Learners who favor the sensing function like to see, touch, and work with real objects, those that engage the senses.

  > Videos, photographs, or drawings are not as helpful as the real object, but are more helpful than written descriptions.

- Learners who are more intuitive appreciate the novel, the unusual– material that involves the imagination.

  > Art forms, poetry, music, and fiction have the potential to intrigue the intuitive person.

Of course, the subject in which we work also determines the kinds of materials we use. I am not suggesting that we regularly read poetry to a group of mechanics in training. Nevertheless, an occasion may arise when a poem is relevant, or perhaps an excerpt from Stephen King's *Christine*. The point is that we must try to bring in learning materials that connect with psychological preferences other than thinking.

Developing Learning Style

As I mention earlier in this chapter, we should encourage students to develop alternative learning styles, as well as try to use methods and materials that are congruent with their preferred style. Experienced students are usually adept at learning in a variety of ways even though they still have preferences. Rather than the result of a conscious, deliberate process, it is more likely that people who have been students for a long time have learned to adapt to a variety of teaching styles in order to be successful. What we can do is to help make this development overt.

If people are to develop different learning styles consciously, they first must be aware of the styles they use. A formal assessment can be done—many such inventories are now available online and most are quick to administer and easy to interpret (for example, see www.learningstyles.com). Alternatively, we can simply tell students about different learning styles, as most people will recognize themselves from a short description.

I realize that it is neither possible nor appropriate to spend a lot of time talking about learning styles when students are there for a different subject. However, being aware of the variety of ways people learn can become a part of the atmosphere through brief and regular references to individual differences. It is easy to say, "Now for those of you who like to see the real thing, I've brought in a carburetor." Or, "For the creative crowd, here's an unusual little poem about being an electrician." It takes just a minute and may connect with a person.

Students develop learning preferences by being exposed to them, through what we do as teachers, and through understanding the differences among their peers. Perhaps more importantly, they develop new styles by having the opportunity to try learning in a new way while being conscious of doing so. The experience must feel safe and comfortable. No one in the room should stereotype ("Of course you are a feeling type, so you wouldn't get this") or joke about differences. Also, no one should be forced to try anything they do not wish to try. I know I would quickly leave a situation where anyone tried to make me sing or even hum a tune. At the same time, some challenge is essential; to achieve this is a delicate balance. Usually we can sense when the time is not right to push as opposed to the time when a gentle nudge will make the difference. Being aware of this is essential.

Summary

For this chapter, I chose to use psychological type theory as a basis for understanding learning styles. Many other approaches (e.g. Kolb's (1984) Learning Style Inventory) are commonly used to provide valuable information for educators and learners alike. I would encourage anyone who is especially interested in learning style to explore alternatives. Psychological type preferences include introversion, an inner focus, extraversion, a focus on the external world, thinking, a logical way of making judgments, feeling, a values-based way of making judgments, sensing, a reliance on the five senses, and intuition, a reliance on images and visions.

We need to consider learners' preferences when we structure our teaching. Some people need a clear outline; others are more comfortable with going with the flow. The best compromise is to include both planned and intuitive aspects in the learning environment. Similarly, when we select teaching methods and learning materials, we need to be aware of learning styles. There are two goals here—one to match what we do to student preferences, the other to expand the ways in which people can learn by exposing them to alternative methods and materials. To help students develop other styles, we have to first help them become aware of their preferences, then give them opportunities to experience other options.

Chapter Six

Establishing Relationships

Last summer, as I have done every summer for nearly 20 years, I worked with a group of new community college instructors who were learning about teaching, meeting from 8:00 a.m. to 1:00 p.m. over three weeks. This particular group was composed mostly of tradespeople. During our last week, I exchanged classes with a colleague teaching another group in the same program. His students wanted to meet me since I had written our text, and I thought it would be interesting for my gang to experience a different teaching style. During this exchange, I found that I was intensely curious about what my colleague was doing with *my* students. I even went so far as to look into the classroom. That evening, while writing in my teaching journal, I realized that I felt something like jealousy, and the next day I told the students about this reaction, although I did not use the word "jealousy" in my comments. One young man said in an *in sotto* voice to another, "What's she talking about?" His classmate responded, "She thinks we were cheatin' on her." I blushed, and we all laughed.

We develop relationships with learners during any teaching and learning interaction. Unless we happen to be among the unfortunate souls who lecture to groups of 500 people, teaching is about relationships. Different educators, perhaps because of their personality or philosophy of teaching, develop different kinds of relationships with their students, but a relationship it is. My particular anecdote may appall someone who prefers a more distant relationship with students, but this is my way of being a teacher, and both ways are valid. I experience this caring relationship even in an online course where I never meet the students in person. Other people would say they respect their students. Some may describe their students as colleagues or potential colleagues. One educator I interviewed recently was clear as to where she drew the line: she was friendly but never friends with students.

In this chapter, I first suggest we become cognizant of the kind of relationship we prefer to have with learners. We need to be clear about this in our own minds. I then describe three different kinds of teacher-learner relationships and give suggestions how to establish these early on in a course or workshop.

How do We Relate to Learners?

The way in which we relate to learners depends in large part on our personality and tends to echo how we generally relate to others. Authentic teachers are basically the same in the classroom as they are in other aspects of their lives. An introverted person who does not like to reveal much to others would not be likely to tell personal stories in class. An educator who enjoys the logical thinking required by a discipline or thinks it is most important to focus on the practical skills required by a trade would tend to relate to students through the subject matter. This person would see students as colleagues or potential colleagues since they share a mutual interest in the content of the course, program, or workshop. Finally, a person who loves to make friends and welcomes a large social circle would be more likely to develop close, warm relationships with students.

The way we relate to learners also depends on our individual concept of the role of teachers. We all have assumptions and beliefs about how teachers should behave. These built-in assumptions may have been absorbed from our culture, community or the institution for which we work, and shape our own philosophy of teaching. For example, it is traditional in some cultures and communities to respect and look up to the teacher. A more familiar relationship between student and teacher would be perceived as inappropriate in that context. Even the way that educators expect learners to address them–by title or by first name–reflects their assumptions. Such practices vary from place to place and institution to institution.

Factors such as age, gender, experience, and the nature of our experience also influence how we relate to students. Less-experienced educators may feel the need to establish credibility by maintaining a more formal role. Some young women to whom I have talked express concern that being too friendly or open will mark them as "pushovers." Other women do not wish to appear to be nurturing or motherly as they object to that common characterization of women. Experienced educators tend to lose their concern about credibility and stereotyping and are more able just to be themselves in their relationships with students. In addition, the nature of our experience plays a part in determining how we relate. For example, if we have taught in a traditional, formal workplace, we will behave differently than if we have taught in a more collaborative environment.

Last of all, to some extent the subject in which we work has an impact on how we relate to learners. The study of mathematics or forestry management does not naturally involve warm, caring relationships, whereas developmental psychology, early childhood education, or counseling do. I have also observed a correlation between gender, subject, and the nature of relationships. In trades programs where the teacher and the majority of the students are male and the content is skills-based, a special kind of camaraderie exists. In other subjects, such as nursing or early childhood care where the groups are mostly composed of women, teaching and learning is often more collaborative, nurturing, and centered in relationships.

Our responses to a simple set of questions may help to make explicit what kind of relationship we prefer.

- Am I reluctant to reveal personal aspects of my life to others?

- Am I more comfortable with defined boundaries around the various facets of my life?

- Am I more interested in discussing my discipline with others than getting to know them personally?

- Do I feel more responsible for educating professionals or training people to do a job than for shaping the person himself or herself?

- Do I value warm, caring relationships in my work?

- Do I see myself as having a role in helping others in their personal lives?

"Yes" responses to the first two questions point to a preference for maintaining a respectful distance with students. "Yes" responses to the next two questions direct us to collegial relationships. And, "yes" responses to the last two questions mean we are likely to prefer close relationships with students.

A Respectful Distance

Our usual tendency is to regard the position of educator with respect and to expect that some distance will be maintained. The position of educator inevitably carries with it a certain amount of authority and power. Learners do not expect to become friends with their teachers in most situations. By simply not stepping over those existing boundaries ourselves, we can maintain a relationship of respectful distance. In such a relationship, the focus is on the subject. Students may never know if we are married or single or have a dog or a cat, and it does not matter that they do not know.

This relationship is not cold or uncaring. We are enthusiastic about the content and very interested in our students' learning, including any problems they may be having. A distant, respectful relationship does not limit discussion, interaction, or working with students. Nor does it constrain us from encouraging critical reflection and the questioning of assumptions. What marks it is that the educator and the learner remain uninvolved with each other's personal lives. For those who do not like to reveal themselves to others in general or distrust quick intimacy, this is a natural style. It fits well in teaching contexts where the subject itself is impersonal. Here are some ways in which we can establish a relationship of respectful distance.

- Relate to students primarily through the subject; that is, discuss and work with the content of the course.

- Demonstrate interest in and concern for student learning.

- Demonstrate personal enthusiasm for the subject.

- Share anecdotes from our professional lives, but not from our personal lives.

- Gently refer students who come with personal problems to a counselor or other individual more able to deal with that aspect of student development.

- Choose to be addressed by a title, Ms., Mr., Prof., or Dr., although this is certainly not necessary in such a relationship.

Collegial Relationships

Educators who are involved in professional training or in-service workshops often regard what they do as working with colleagues. For example, a nursing instructor who is in charge of a group of practicing nurses on their way to becoming nurse practitioners would see herself involved in a collegial relationship with her students. Similarly, a management consultant leading sessions with company personnel on issues such as conflict resolution, teamwork, or staff-manager relations would find himself in a collegial relationship with participants. People teaching others to be carpenters, computer programmers, scientists, graphic designers, engineers, and craftspeople could view their students as future colleagues and establish this kind of connection with them from the beginning.

While a collegial relationship has the discipline as its basis, it also involves the educator and students working collaboratively as co-learners. Due to mutual professional interests and experience, less separation and more closeness exist between educator and learner than in the respectfully distant relationship. The collegial relationship builds on the sharing of experience and expertise as both the educator and the learner have valuable knowledge and skills to contribute. The more experience students have in the field, the clearer the collegial relationship is, but it is also possible to establish such a relationship with novices in the subject. I give some ideas for doing so here.

- Establish the shared professional or discipline-related goals with learners through discussion or group activities.

- Explore values and beliefs related to the subject area that are held in common between teacher and students.

- Question learners' professional goals and values and encourage them to question ours.

- Describe and rely on our experience in the subject, trade, or profession and ask students to do the same.

- Illustrate and provide examples by drawing on our experience and ask students to contribute examples from their experience.

- Call on the experience and expertise of participants as much and as often as possible.

- Work with learners to understand the content.

- Learn from our students while they learn from us.

Close Relationships

In a close relationship, we come to know our students as people and encourage them to know us. This does not mean that we tell students deeply personal things or share our own problems in an inappropriate way. It is the creation of an atmosphere of openness and availability. We are also people with a life outside of the classroom or seminar room, and we do not draw a sharp line between who we are as educators and who we are as people.

Some educators prefer close, open, and personal relationships with students because of their own nature, their philosophy of teaching, or the subject area within which they work. In my own practice, I work with people who are already adult educators and those who will become educators. Some of our goals include increasing self-awareness, developing values, questioning personal beliefs and assumptions, and learning how we engage in relationships with others. In these circumstances, it would be difficult for me to maintain a distant relationship with my students. That I choose a close relationship over a collegial relationship has to do with how I prefer to work with people. There are many such settings in adult education—settings where the emphasis is on working with others. A close relationship between educator and learner and among learners definitely facilitates that process.

Establishing a close relationship with students involves some risks; no one who finds it uncomfortable should attempt it. Less experienced educators should move slowly in this direction. It is possible to inadvertently create dependencies or to set up expectations that go beyond what we intend. We should be very clear in our own minds about what we are doing and where our boundaries are. In my 25 years of practice, I have only encountered two or three occasions where a student misinterpreted my intentions or an unhealthy dependency occurred.

Given this caveat, here are some of the things I suggest to help foster a close relationship with students.

- Use our first names and tell students we prefer to be addressed that way.

- Be accessible outside of the classroom and encourage students to come to our office or meet us in the cafeteria.

- Give students our e-mail address and, if we are comfortable in doing so, our phone number and assure them we enjoy hearing from them.

- Use examples and illustrations from our own personal lives when appropriate.

- Refer to where we live, our children, pets, or hobbies in ordinary conversation.

- Ask students to share their experiences in journals or autobiographies.

- Regularly use humor and stories.

- Be receptive to helping students with problems and issues when it is appropriate and possible.

- Follow up with students, asking if they need help or are feeling comfortable with the learning situation.

Summary

Whether we are explicit about it or not, we all develop some kind of a relationship with learners. Teaching is a communicative process–it is about people working together to foster learning–and that means relationships develop. Rather than leave this critical aspect of teaching to chance, we need to think about what kind of an association we have or want to have with our students. The relationships we choose to develop depend on many factors, including our own personality, how we interpret the role of teacher, our experience, the context within which we work, and the subject we teach.

I describe three possible kinds of relationships, though of course there are many variations on these and probably several other categories. My point is not to develop a comprehensive taxonomy of relationships but to bring us to awareness of the different ways in which we do work with students. We can consciously create the kind of relationship we prefer. To this end, I provide some suggestions for facilitating each kind of relationship.

When we establish a respectful distance with learners, we focus on the subject and do not become involved with each other's lives. We stay in the role of teacher as traditionally defined. In a collegial relationship, we step toward being a co-learner. Students and teacher alike share experiences, expertise, knowledge, and skills, and learn from each other. A close relationship between educator and learners leads us to know each other as people, to learn about each other's lives, values, and beliefs. Although it can be risky, it also can be the most satisfying of relationships in teaching.

Chapter Seven

Organizing Sessions

I remember a university professor who taught me European literature when I was 18 years old. Of the many teachers I have had, this man stays vividly in my mind. He shuffled into the classroom, usually late, trailing coffee-stained papers and dropping cigarette ashes. He usually forgot what novel we were discussing until someone reminded him. Then he might or might not have his copy of the book with him. We learned never to give him our only copy of an essay, for the chances were good he would lose it. He paid no attention to when the class was supposed to end, only noticing finally that everyone was leaving to go to another class. In this course, I came to love European literature deeply. Despite his peculiarities, this teacher had such strong passion for his subject that no student was untouched.

I am not advocating this approach as a model for others to follow. I do not imagine that anyone could replicate his style. The point of introducing my eccentric but beloved professor is to emphasize that well-planned organization is not necessarily the key to good teaching. As mentioned in Chapter Five, some educators prefer a more intuitive approach to teaching rather than a planned approach, and both can be effective. This chapter contains suggestions for organizing learning sessions, but not every suggestion will be right for every teacher.

The ideas that follow include:

- using agendas
- providing an overview of what is to come
- introducing sessions
- changing pace
- flowing from one activity to another
- summarizing periodically
- clarifying relationships among topics
- bringing a session to a close

Using Agendas

An agenda is helpful for both participants and educator. For those participants who like clear structure, an agenda prepares them for what is going to happen, and for the educator, it provides a guide for managing time.

- I use a very simple agenda for a class, a numbered list of what will occur. The list might include, for example,

    1. Any comments from last week?

    2. Large group discussion of reading on moral development.

    3. Group work: exchanging incidents related to moral issues.

    4. Next week: ego development.

- A more detailed agenda is helpful for a one-time workshop.

    People particularly appreciate it when times are indicated on the agenda for a full-day session.

- The agenda may be photocopied and handed out to each student or posted on chart paper or a whiteboard.

- As important as it is to have an agenda of some kind, it is equally important to know when to drop it.

  > When the discussion is enthusiastic, a different topic arises, or participants express a need to move off in another direction, I revise the agenda.

- In this case, for those who want structure, we need to be very clear that we are deviating from the original plan.

  > It is a simple matter to say, "I get the impression we need to spend more time on this topic. Why don't we leave out the next group activity so we can continue this discussion?" However, be sure not to react to only one or two learners. Watch faces and body language carefully to get a sense of what the whole group prefers.

Providing Overviews

I use an agenda to provide an overview of what is going to happen throughout a class or workshop.

- To make their plans even more explicit and detailed, some educators explain the purpose, goals, and objectives of the session, and how it will relate to other topics.

- Some writers advocate the use of "advance organizers," a kind of framework or structure onto which students can hang the various topics under discussion.

  > This might consist of a chart or drawing that shows how the topics to be discussed are related to each other or, more simply, the same information provided verbally. The technique appeals to the intuitive learner who likes to see the whole picture and the thinking

learner who enjoys establishing the underlying relationships among topics.

Introducing Sessions

An agenda or an overview (or both) may introduce most learning sessions. However at times we need a little more.

- In situations where learners come to a session in the evening after a full day of work, as is common in adult education practice, giving people a chance to relax, unwind, say hello to each other, and make the transition from work to learning is appreciated.

- In a short-term workshop, especially where people do not know each other, a warm-up activity is often helpful (see Chapter One for more information).

- In a course that is ongoing over several sessions, it is important to give participants an opportunity to remember what they were doing the previous day or week, as well to help them leave their day behind and turn to learning.

- The simplest way to open a session is to ask for comments, questions, and reactions to the previous class.

    > This approach also elicits feedback for the educator in the form of participant response. I make this introduction low-key and informal–students should not feel that they are required to recall points or that their comments will be evaluated. Sometimes, this technique will spark a ten- or fifteen-minute discussion; at other times, no response will occur. If silence is the usual reaction, it is time to try another approach. However, do not give up too quickly:

people do not always have something to say or may simply be gathering their thoughts or reflecting on the content of the last class.

- Some educators keep a teaching journal or log, which can be used as an interesting way of introducing sessions in an ongoing course.

> I select excerpts from my journal, no more than one page in length, and hand these out at the beginning of the next class. During the quiet time that follows while people read, these excerpts serve to review what happened previously and give some idea of the teacher's perspective on the session. In my experience, journal excerpts stimulate excellent discussion and draw people back into the learning atmosphere.

Changing Pace

Each learning group develops its own unique style. Some groups are talkative, outgoing, and enthusiastic. Others are quiet. In some groups, a struggle emerges until people establish norms of behavior and come to know each other. In other groups, such problems as the presence of a few individuals who dominate the conversation or others who contribute little are never satisfactorily resolved. In any group, whatever its character, it is important to not get stuck in a rut, that is, proceed in the same way at the same rate every day. Habits and patterns develop early and easily, and are hard to break. Building a change of pace into the organization of the session helps avoid a monotonous pace.

- As a rule, within each session I alternate between times of active engagement and quieter activity; this may simply involve students listening, watching, reflecting, or working individually.

> A continual diet of intense group work is tiring and begins to lose its effect; a long monologue or extensive observation leaves learners passive, uninvolved, and inattentive.

- Moving back and forth between discussion, mini-lectures, group work, videos or slides or demonstrations, and practical activities not only keeps everyone interested, but also meets the needs of people with different learning styles (see Chapter Five).

- In some situations, we need to consider physical needs in organizing the pacing of a session.

> For example, in a full-day session, a quiet time right after lunch is not a good idea. People get sleepy after lunch and need to be active to stay motivated. Similarly, in an evening class, 9:00 p.m. is not a good time to introduce a new topic or give a talk on a theoretical point. Place discussion, group work, role-plays, and skits after lunch, later in the evening, or first thing on Monday morning. Groups vary, though, and we need to read each group to learn their special rhythm.

Creating Flow

How do we organize a session so that one thing flows gracefully into the next? We all know those awkward moments—when discussion fizzles out after a few minutes; when one group completes an activity in five minutes and other groups are just getting underway; when we plan time for questions and there are none; when participants cannot seem to figure out what they are doing or why. All of us have experienced such problems, which are best faced with openness and humor. It is far better to say, "I guess I misjudged your interest in this discussion!" than try to cover up what we perceive as a mistake.

- Creating a natural flow between events comes more easily with experience and practice. However, there are some things we can do within the organization of the session that will help. We need to make the links clear between each part of a session so that the students grasp the flow we have in mind.

  > Opening remarks or detailed agendas will help make this apparent.

- However, at the same time, we must be flexible and open to change. We must be prepared and able to swerve from our course.

- When the group clearly demonstrates a new or divergent interest, if it is germane, we can use the obvious enthusiasm to generate further discussion, linking it to our main topic.

- We have to learn to read the mood of each group and attend to the signals of body language—the diverted eyes, the twisting in the chair, the rifling through papers, the glances at the clock—that tell us it is time to move on.

- We can plan options in case the discussion does not go as we expect or there is less interest in a certain area than we thought.

  > For example, we can have in reserve several additional probing questions to recharge a discussion, extra overheads to arouse interest in a topic, or more

material ready than we think will be needed to allow
for a graceful exit.

- Finally, we need to stay relaxed and positive ourselves, as hard as that may be at times, and realize that what may seem to us as a boulder in the flowing stream can go virtually unnoticed by students.

> Observing the group and being in tune with their rhythm is the key to maintaining flow; how to describe the ways in which this is accomplished is difficult. I continually scan the room, even in a large group or a workshop with strangers. I look at facial expressions, the way people are sitting, whether or not they whisper to each other. I listen to voice tone, I try to read what lies behind what they say. I am prepared in my mind to shift gears at any moment.

Summarizing Periodically

Providing periodic summaries is another way to direct the flow of a session. In addition, summaries help students keep track of where things are in the session and follow the overall structure. A good summary of a discussion highlights the points raised and helps people distinguish between major concepts and minor side issues. In a summary, ideas are usually expressed in a slightly different way, which may illuminate matters for someone who has a different learning style. And not everyone listens carefully all the time; a summary offers a review and gives people an opportunity to pick up any points they may have missed.

- Present summaries in the natural breaks in the flow of the session.

  > For example, when a discussion winds down or at the end of a group activity is always a good summary spot. Sometimes a summary in the middle of a discussion will help focus things or bring people back on track.

- Summarize if participants seem bewildered or confused.

- Although it varies with the circumstances, I try consciously to summarize at least once per hour. However, too many summaries can become boring.

- Summaries should not be long—a few sentences are usually adequate.

- Ask students to take on the task of summarizing.

  > This is a helpful technique for fostering student responsibility for learning (see Chapter Four). There are different ways of doing this. Students can take turns summarizing so that they know who is responsible for which summary. Alternatively, we can simply ask, "Who would like to summarize this discussion?" Of course, students should know in advance that someone would be doing the summaries. This quickly becomes a group norm and works well.

Clarifying Relationships Among Topics

One purpose of providing summaries is to clarify relationships among topics within a session, but there are other ways of doing this as well. As educators, we usually have considerable experience and expertise in the subject we are working with. To us, how concepts and issues are interconnected is clear, but to a student with less knowledge, this may not be the case. It depends on the characteristics of the learners; in some cases, participants are well versed in the discipline, and clarifying relationships among topics is less important. I often teach a course on research methods in the same term as I teach an adult education course. In the latter, participants are mostly experienced educators; in the former, almost no one has any experience doing research. It is much more important that I ensure the relationships among topics are clear in the research course.

- When introducing a new concept, it is a good idea to mention briefly how that concept relates to topics that have already been discussed.

  > This need not be complex; a simple comment will suffice.

- Sometimes a concept map or a chart of the topics and their interrelationships is very useful.

  > I often have participants generate such a map in a group activity. For example, I might give the groups a set of index cards each with a key concept written on it. I ask people to arrange the cards to show how the concepts are related and then post their arrangement on the wall. We circulate around the room to look at the relationships depicted and discuss the differences.

- Another technique is to list the concepts and ask people to produce a drawing of any kind to show the relationships among them.

  > This latter activity can yield very creative results. Last summer, a group of trades' instructors were producing drawings to illustrate the relationship between instrumental, communicative, and emancipatory knowledge. A drawing of a tree showed instrumental knowledge as the root or foundation, the trunk as communicative learning, and the branches and leaves as emancipatory learning. Similarly, drawings of bicycles and teeter-totters demonstrated different

conceptualizations of how these kinds of knowledge build on each other.

We were all extremely pleased with our work, and I am sure that most of those participants remember their drawings and consequently how those terms are connected.

Coming to a Close

I have seen classes where students rush out at the scheduled end of class even as their teacher is in mid-sentence. Every learning session needs an official close, however brief. There are a variety of ways of doing this.

- A simple close is to offer a short summary and comment on the next class.

   "Today, we talked about how to prepare the soil. Tomorrow, we will go on to discuss planting and watering."

- Closing with a provocative or challenging question is sometimes effective.

   "Today, we talked about experimental research designs. Do you think control groups are ethical in educational research? Think about this for next class."

- In workshops and sometimes in classes, ask participants to take five minutes to consider and record something they will do differently in their practice because of the session.

- Similarly, hand out blank index cards and ask people to write down the most significant thing they have learned on one side of the card and one question that has arisen on the other.

   Either collect the cards or ask students to keep them, and use these responses to introduce the next class.

- Ask participants to do a quick drawing depicting how they felt about the session or to write down one word or phrase to describe their reaction.

> I tend to vary how I close a session depending on my reading of the group's reaction. For example, if I think people may be confused, I will ask them to write down a question. If everyone seems up and excited, I end with a provocative question.

Summary

Organizing a learning session has many facets. Each educator needs to find an organizational strategy that is comfortable for him or her. Some people find agendas too constricting; others find summaries boring. Nevertheless, most students require some visible organizational framework, especially when the subject is unfamiliar to them.

Agendas both help people keep track of what is happening and let them know what to expect next. An overview gives students the framework for the concepts and ideas to come. In introducing a session, it is useful to link the material to come to the content of the previous class in order to ensure that people recall what is necessary and anticipate what is next. They will then be comfortable and ready to participate.

Each learning session should include a change of pace—periods of intense involvement followed by a quieter time for reflection. Orchestrating the flow of a class or workshop takes some practice; we need to be flexible and pay attention to the mood of the group. Periodic summaries highlight points and help students connect one idea to another. Relationships among topics can be clarified through simple verbal comments or charts and maps that are more complex. Finally, it is important to end a learning session in a meaningful way—with a summary, a question, or by giving people the opportunity to communicate how they felt.

Chapter Eight

Managing Time

Probably all of us have attended a session where the educator had ten or twenty points still to present and only a few minutes remaining. Whether they rush through or abandon the items, we end up feeling frustrated. Why did they ramble on so long at the beginning when there was so much material to cover? Why did they allow discussion to wander so far afield with so many concepts still to introduce? Managing time in a learning session can be difficult, especially for the less experienced educator. How do we know how long a discussion will last? Or, how long an activity will take? What happens if we plan to talk for ten minutes, then answer questions for twenty minutes, and there are no questions?

As I was thinking about this chapter, I was preparing a session that was to be video-conferenced to a university in Mexico. In video conferencing, people are physically located at different sites, and a video of them speaking is broadcast across sites. Participants in the session were physically located in several sites in Mexico; the timing needed to be exact. I rather arbitrarily settled on 40 minutes for a short presentation and discussion of adult education strategies. English was everyone's second language. People were intimidated by the video-conferencing technology as well as by me since they had one of my books as a text. I had not thought of these factors in advance, but I certainly thought of them as I waited for the questions and comments from the participants and the 40 minutes began to feel like four hours. The program facilitator filled in with comments of her own and did an outstanding job of encouraging her students to join the discussion, but I certainly was reminded how delicate and complex managing time can be. In this example, time management was inhibited by language, culture, and the technology, but I'm sure we have all had similar experiences in a variety of settings.

Having a well-organized session helps us to manage time effectively (see Chapter Seven). However, the process seems somewhat intuitive. Perhaps it is the tacit knowledge that comes with experience—the kind of thing we just seem to do instinctively after many years in the classroom without being able to articulate it. I find myself thinking deeply about just what it is that I do as I write this chapter. I first present some factors that may influence timing. I then discuss managing time in relation to three types of strategies: presenting material, leading discussion, and facilitating group work.

Influences on Timing

Many factors influence how time passes in a learning session, some of which we do not recognize, others of which we cannot control. Even in the same group, from one occasion to another, wide variations occur in how long things take. For example, if the one or two individuals who usually lead off a discussion have had a bad day and are tired, this will have an impact on everyone's participation and hence on the timing.

- Take into consideration the background and experience of participants with the subject when thinking about managing time.

    > People who have little knowledge of the field are likely to have less to say than those that have considerable expertise.

    > If the group is mixed, the more experienced participants will likely carry the discussion.

- Consider the students' educational experience, which is perhaps even more important than their familiarity with the discipline.

    > For example, participants who are comfortable taking courses, engaging in discussion, asking questions, and working collaboratively carry those attributes into any learning session.

    > On the other hand, if participants' previous experience is with a different style of learning, they may well be apprehensive and remain quiet.

- Always consider the learners' interest in the topic; interested students have more to say, less interested students have less to say.

    > Even when learners choose the topics for a course (see Chapter Three), they will not have an equal interest in every topic. In a workshop, people attend for a variety of reasons, some of which have little to do with the content. For example, they may be meeting the expectations of a supervisor, gaining needed credits, or simply escaping their routine. When participants are less interested in what is happening, there are many things we can do to spark interest, but in the meantime, time management is affected.

- The verbal facility of the participants also can be a factor, especially when many of the participants are struggling with another language.

  > As I noticed in the videoconference with Mexican participants, people working in a second language are more reluctant to speak out or to make long contributions. It probably does not happen very often that we work with a group in our mother tongue while they all speak another language, but when it does occur, this needs to be considered in our timing. We need to speak more slowly; learners will speak less. Even when there are some students using their second language, we need to consider our timing.

- The time of day of the learning session can influence participation and hence time management.

  > Evening sessions, when people are tired, may be less lively than daytime sessions. We need to be prepared to cut down on our expectations for what is accomplished.

- The room set-up is another factor to consider.

  > For example, a crowded or overheated classroom affects everyone, including the instructor, slowing the pace and diminishing what is accomplished.

> I once led a workshop for about 50 adult educators where I found myself in a very wide and shallow room. No matter where I stood or sat, I could not see everyone. Given the shape of the room and the number of people packed into it, I also could not walk around. And, to finish things off, it was a hot summer day, and there was no air conditioning. The feedback at the end of the day indicated that some people found the session "slow," and the pace "dragging." My time management was clearly influenced by the setting in which I was working.

Presenting Information

When we present information through a lecture, demonstration, or video, we control the timing more easily than when we use other teaching strategies. We know exactly, or at least approximately, how long the presentation will take and can watch the time. This does not mean, of course, that we ignore the students' reactions, questions, and looks of confusion. Educators with less experience usually worry about running out of things to say and facing time unfilled. To compensate for this, they may prepare far too much material, then feel obligated to use all of it. Rehearsal does not seem to help. It is very different to present something to a group of learners than to the mirror, our spouse, or our loyal dog. Managing time effectively in the classroom or workshop only comes with practice. To improve timing try some of these suggestions.

- Prepare an outline, written in as much detail as needed.

    This can be the same agenda that is given to students and can include reminders, examples, and notes to ourselves.

- Do a rough estimate of timing on one copy of the outline, noting how long each point or topic may take.

    Keeping track of the time as we talk or demonstrate is important. It is useful to notice how long each point is taking and how accurate our estimates are. This allows for ongoing adjustment.

- Mark the halfway point in a presentation on the outline—at this point, half of the time should be gone.

- Know what to leave out or add in order to adjust the timing as necessary.

> Marking things that can be deleted and preparing optional material to add is best done in advance for the less-experienced educator but can usually be done as we go with practice.

- Remember that most participants do not mind if a session ends a few minutes early.

Leading Discussion

Managing time during a discussion can be tricky. How long a discussion remains animated and interesting depends on many factors, including aspects of participants' lives from outside the learning setting. With practice, we develop a sense of the rhythm of discussions that helps with the timing, but it is not easy to articulate just what this "sense" is made up of. In Chapter Ten, I write in more detail about how to facilitate a good discussion, and timing is a part of that. Here are a few suggestions.

- Prepare a long list of specific discussion questions.

> Asking people to "discuss Chapter Two" does not lead to much. I always have more questions than I think I will use, so that if some of the questions do not stimulate good conversation, I move on to another.

- Plan roughly how much time to spend on each discussion question.

> For example, if I am planning an hour-long discussion, I might expect to discuss four different issues, each one for approximately fifteen minutes. In that case, I would have about eight questions prepared.

- Let the conversation continue if good discussion results from any one question.

> If people are talking enthusiastically with each other, raising good points, and asking interesting questions, ignore preplanned time estimates and mentally discard other discussion questions. At the same time, continually watch the clock. We might feel, for example, that two of our four questions are essential to discuss, or three of four. We can adjust the timing accordingly.

- Introduce another question as soon as the discussion flags.

> Some silence is good in a discussion, but there is a point where it no longer means that people are reflecting–it means the topic is over. As well as watching people's body language, interpreting their tone of voice, and attending to the content of what they say, we simultaneously must watch the clock. If discussion flags after only five minutes, we need to go on and mentally add another discussion question to the agenda, or perhaps just wait and see if the next topic will be the one to catch people's interest.

Facilitating Group Work

One major worry of educators in managing time during group work is that one or two groups will finish earlier than the others and have "nothing to do." Barbara Gross Davis (1993) in *Tools for Teaching* recommends that if 25% of the groups are finished an activity, other groups should be told they have five more minutes–the 25/5 rule, she calls it. I am afraid that you would then have three out of four groups rushing through their work. In my experience, it is rare for students to have "nothing to do." They may have finished the discussion and exercise suggested, but will continue to talk about the issues raised or other issues related to the content, or perhaps topics from their professional lives. These are all valid things to do.

Based on my participation in workshops where not enough time was allotted for activities and having experienced extreme frustration when yanked back to the large group, I would much rather err on the side of allowing too much time than too little.

It is useful to work out rough estimates for the timing of group work, but rather than risk rushing people, I suggest that we prepare an optional activity or discussion should things go more quickly than we anticipated. It is also important to plan time for discussing the results of group work or debriefing.

In Chapter Fourteen, I write about how to foster learning through group work. Here, I give some suggestions related to managing time during group work.

- Be aware that the more small groups there are, the longer everything takes.

    In a large group of 60, for example, we might have 15 small groups of four. Just getting into and out of the groups takes more time than we might expect.

- Prepare rough time estimates; they can be helpful.

    However, unlike many educators, I do not tell participants how long the group work should take (see Chapter Four). I prefer that it take as long as is needed to engage meaningfully in the task. When people ask, "How long do we have?" I respond, "As long as it takes." At first, this frustrates some, but as soon as people see that I mean it, they relax and enjoy the group learning.

- Assess each group's progress at your estimated halfway point.

    It is not a good idea to hover over groups, but walking around the room usually gives an idea of where everyone is. If not, we can ask, "Where are you? How far along are you?"

- Encourage slower groups to finish their work when the majority of other groups will be finished.

    When there is a sense that most groups are coming to the end (sometimes the room grows quieter, or there is a subtle shift in the atmosphere), we can go around again and say, "Will you be finished shortly?" At this time if some groups are not nearly ready, they will say so, and we can readjust the timing.

- Reconvene the larger group.

    At the end of the group work, go around again and ask the groups to reconvene as a whole.

- Allow sufficient time to discuss the results of group work with the full class.

    Sometimes, this involves asking each small group to report on what they did; other times, we may want to take examples from the small groups (especially if there are many of them). Still other times, it is more important to discuss the actual process of collaboration that occurred than what the participants talked about.

- Follow these general guidelines even if the entire group is very large, though it is more difficult.

    I have resorted to flicking lights on and off to bring people back into a large group. We may not always have the opportunity to check with each group, but spot checking is fine.

Summary

Managing teaching time is an elusive process: it is hard to pin down how to do it since it involves managing not only time itself, but also a whole group of people participating in events during that time. Unless we take total control of the situation and dictate the time spent on each thing (which I definitely do not recommend), many factors will influence how the timing of a learning session goes. Characteristics of the participants, such as their background in the subject area and their experience being students, have a strong impact on how much time things take. Even time of day and the nature of the room sometimes matter.

When we present information, we can plan more precisely how much time is needed than when we lead discussions or facilitate group work. Using a well-thought-out agenda and keeping careful track of the time as we proceed will help. In leading discussions, time management depends on how involved people become in the topics. It is always a good idea to have many more discussion questions than we expect to use and continually watch the clock, adjusting and readjusting as we go. In facilitating group work, it is crucial for groups to have enough time to engage meaningfully in the exercise. Helpful strategies are to have rough time estimates in mind and to monitor unobtrusively how far along the groups are.

Managing time effectively comes primarily through practice. Many of the suggestions I make in this chapter become second nature with experience.

Chapter Nine

Selecting Readings

One of our first considerations when planning a course is to decide which readings to use. Is there a potential textbook? Do we already have resources for the topics that might be included? I have even caught myself listing topics based on readings I have easily available on my shelf rather than the other way around. Why do we accept the existence of a strong connection between reading and learning? Are we assuming no learning occurs without reading? Isn't it the case that learning through reading is only one approach, which appeals only to individuals with a particular learning style (see Chapter Five)?

When I look through the literature on adult education strategies, I discover that rarely is there any discussion or questioning of the use of readings. In this chapter, I first pose the question, "Why use readings?" and then go on to review a variety of aspects to consider when we do use readings.

Why Use Readings?

Before the invention of the printing press in the mid-fifteenth century, knowledge in the form of the printed word was accessible only to a few. It really was not until the 1800s that the technology of printing progressed to a point that everyone had access to text and literacy became a requirement for full participation in society. The roots of adult education lie in that early literacy movement. At that time adult educators were viewed as subversive agents responsible for encouraging people to seize the power of knowledge by becoming literate. Perhaps this history explains our strong belief in learning through reading.

By no means do I wish to belittle the importance and power of the written word. The knowledge that became available, for example, to the ordinary person with the first "penny press" in New York in 1833 cannot be overvalued. What I do want to do here is reflect on why we use written material for virtually everything we teach. As the norm, the tradition, it needs to be questioned. Before we run to the photocopier with our stack of articles, we should ask if this is the best way for people to learn this content.

The printed word is an abstract representation of meaning. If we think, for example, of teaching someone to repair an engine, the engine itself is the concrete real thing. A drawing or a photograph of the engine is a two-dimensional representation of it. A written description is an abstract representation. The further we move away from the real thing, the more we are asking of the learner. On the other hand, if we think of teaching abstract concepts, the written or spoken word is the only means of communication. In deciding whether to use readings, we need to ask ourselves whether this medium provides the most helpful way of representing the content. We should have a good reason for using written material, and not just because the content has always been taught this way.

How Much Reading?

When I see a course outline with a suggested reading list of two or three pages, I wonder if the educator actually expects people to read these "suggestions." Or, are they intended to demonstrate to students that the educator is well read in the subject? There are some circumstances in which long reading lists are appropriate, for example, in graduate level courses where students want to collect reference lists. However, such long lists may intimidate students and create anxiety.

Each reading should be chosen for a specific reason. We should be sure that, for example, if people read this article, they will gain a different point of view, or if people read that book, they will acquire new information about the topic. In other words, we should carefully examine our rationale for each choice.

In deciding on how many readings we will use, we also need to consider our students' lives.

- Do the students have prior experience in school and good reading skills or do they struggle through written material?

- How many other courses are they taking, and how much reading is required in those courses?

- Are the learners part-time students and full-time workers who also may have family and community responsibilities?

If we do not know these things, we need to ask. Generally, in my experience, one good, clear, interesting reading on a topic is far more effective than a long list of books or articles that people cannot possibly get through.

Textbook or Not?

In some settings, especially at colleges and universities, a textbook is commonly assigned as a basic source of information. A textbook is convenient for both students and teacher. Instead of lining up at the photocopier with a handful of articles, we can simply say, "Chapter Five is relevant for next week's discussion." Students have available a coherent, organized presentation of material. If we can find a textbook that clearly meets the needs of the students and is congruent with the content, using it may be a good choice.

On the other hand, there are some disadvantages to consider. Textbooks are ordered before a course starts. If we want students to have some choice of topics, it is difficult to select a text in advance that will include the topics students will choose. In this way, they do restrict the amount of responsibility students can have for their learning.

Textbooks usually present only one perspective, that of the author. Sometimes we can find a book composed of chapters by a variety of authors, each with different outlooks, but this is not typical. If one of our goals is to encourage participants to consider alternative perspectives, a textbook can be limiting. Using a text also may tend to act as a framework for the course; that is, we follow the text rather than the interests of the students and our own idea of the structure of the content. Having a framework can be useful, but it can also be a constraint.

When a good textbook is available, a compromise may be the solution.

- Use some of the readings from the text, supplementing it with a selection of articles that provide alternative perspectives.

- Use the supplemental articles to cover those topics not included in the text if learners are involved in selecting topics.

When there is no clearly appropriate textbook, I recommend using a variety of readings rather than a text that is not quite right.

What on Earth are they Talking About?

> *Secondly, it is astonishingly easy to lose the whole picture while focusing on a single pixel. Some constructionists wish to declare a kind of ownership over the content in which a social problem emerged, with the view that the outrages of times gone by are the same outrages which determine the present. This antiquarian view exists as a veneration for....*
>
> (Hacking, 1999).

As much as I and my colleagues are intrigued by Ian Hacking's excellent book, it would be an inappropriate choice of reading for a novice adult educator.

Academic writing has its own technical language or jargon and style. As experts in our field, this jargon becomes second nature to us. For example, I was surprised when Byron Wall, who publishes this book, mentioned that he hated the word "closure." It is a word that adult educators routinely use, but to him it is jargon. Academics who write books and articles in a field generally use the language of that subject. However, more than the special vocabulary poses problems. The sentence structure and the mode of expression found in academic writing is seen nowhere else. When selecting readings for students, we must be cognizant of the difficulty level posed by the vocabulary and style.

At the same time, it is important that students learn the language of the discipline. After all, jargon is a kind of short-cut form of speech that people working in an area use to communicate with each other. Without it, communication would be awkward and difficult. If an auto mechanic had to describe in terms I could understand the tools he was using or the parts he needed when he was talking to another mechanic, it would be silly at best and dangerous at its worst. A balance must found. Learners need to be introduced to the language of the subject in a way they can follow and understand. Readings intended for experts or written by academics at a very high level are too difficult and frustrating for the novice.

How do we find the appropriate level? Here are several suggestions.

- Try out material in class and gauge the response through discussion or informal testing which will indicate the level of understanding. We can ask our students for their direct feedback. How did they perceive the material?

- Consult with colleagues who teach in the same area to get a second opinion on the suitability of the material. We can also find out what they have found useful in their classes.

- Ask someone who has a similar background to our students to go over the reading and give us an opinion on its difficulty.

Generally, it is better to err on the side of simplicity rather than complexity.

Using Readings to Challenge

One important goal of adult education is to encourage participants to consider a variety of perspectives and to question points of view critically.

- Use readings that contain opposing points of view to stimulate this kind of thinking.

> For example, in a course I facilitated on workplace learning, we first read about the concept of a "learning organization" (Watkins and Marsick, 1993), then read a strong critique of the concept (Fenwick, 1998). Students who initially agreed with the idea of a learning organization subsequently began to question it. Some people maintained their support and went on to apply the concept in their workplace, but others completely changed their opinion.

Not every subject lends itself to this strategy. When the topics are scientific, technical, or focused on detailed information, alternative points of view don't always exist. Still, we need to keep in mind that scientific paradigms do shift, and we can find assumptions and points of view to expose and discuss in any discipline. Also, we can always critically question the basic premise of why it is important to acquire this knowledge. For example, students preparing to be counselors or early childhood specialists can question the assumption that they need to learn about empirical research methods. Readings that challenge the importance or relevance of knowledge can be provocative and invigorating.

Critical thinking is a foundational skill in adult education, even in job preparation programs such as the trades and technologies. This is especially the case given how quickly information, equipment, and procedures change. Students need to learn how to think for themselves, how to be critical of what they read and hear, how to trouble shoot, how to solve problems, and how to find innovative approaches.

Reflecting Diversity in Readings

When the group of learners is diverse, with people from different cultural backgrounds and varying levels of experience and expertise, we can select readings that cater to the interests and needs of the subgroups within the class.

- Provide, for example, a core of basic readings, which everyone uses with additional sets of optional readings focused on special concerns.

- Develop and organize a group of readings into several categories based on their level of difficulty.

Those participants with more experience in a field could choose the more advanced readings if they wished.

- Encourage participants to bring in readings they have found.

    Some people may belong to a professional organization and receive a newsletter relevant to a topic under discussion or subscribe to a journal containing pertinent articles. Even newspaper clippings or advertisements may be appropriate in some subjects. If everyone gets into the habit of looking for and bringing in readings, we soon get the diversity we are looking for.

- Avoid giving extra readings to those students who are already struggling with the content.

    As teachers, we tend to think of more reading as the solution for all ills, but for a person who feels overwhelmed with things as they are, this is not the answer.

Providing Alternative Readings

In some subjects, we can explore alternatives to the traditional academic texts through fiction, poetry, and articles from popular magazines or newspapers. Of course, there are alternatives to the print format altogether, but this chapter is concerned only with printed materials.

- Include a short story to provide a welcome break to the usual reading.

- Include even longer works of fiction when appropriate.

    At Renaissance College, an innovative school affiliated with the University of New Brunswick, Ronald Wright's *A Scientific Romance* was overwhelmingly successful in fostering good critical thinking and discussion. Similarly, Russell Roberts' *The Invisible Heart: An Economic Romance*, provides refreshing alternative perspective on capitalism through the discussions between an economist and a literature teacher who are falling in love.

- Include some materials that appeal to the creative and intuitive learners.

    Poetry may not be to everyone's taste, but in most groups, some will enjoy it. We can find a poem relevant to almost any topic. It can be thought provoking or fun-filled. A humorous poem goes a long way toward creating a good atmosphere in a learning session.

    Similarly, magazine and newspaper articles provide a change of tempo and may present an alternative viewpoint to more academic texts. Again, it is particularly effective if learners get into the habit of bringing such readings to the group.

Using Readings Wisely

It can be very frustrating for students if we ignore what they have spent a couple of hours reading. I tend to be guilty of this in that I sometimes assume people will make the connection between the reading and the class activities or discussion. I treat the reading as background and go from there. Students let me know quickly enough that they resent my neglect of the reading. Here are some ways we can ensure the reading is integrated into group sessions.

- Distribute discussion questions along with the chapter or article to help people focus their reading and then address those questions in the next class.

- Introduce the points for discussion in the session rather than in advance to avoid students reading only to find the "answers" to the questions.

- Ask participants to generate discussion questions in pairs or small groups and present those questions to their classmates.

- Have participants write a sentence or even a word to summarize their reactions to a reading.

- Include time for reading in a class or workshop if appropriate.

- Provide participants with a choice of articles, each with a varying perspective, to read either in class or before class, and then explain the article they read to those who did not read it.

Summary

As educators, many of us have learned our own subject mainly through reading. We associate learning with reading and automatically reach for printed materials when we plan our teaching. While I would never deny the importance of reading, I do suggest that we carefully question why we use readings and be sure we have a good rationale for our choices.

Little is written on how to select readings. In this chapter, I review some issues I believe are important. To put everything we have read ourselves into a reading list is not helpful for students but, on the contrary, is overwhelming and intimidating. Textbooks are convenient but may constrain what we do and provide us with only one perspective. We need to avoid readings that contain unnecessary jargon or an obtuse writing style. Using readings with opposing points of view helps students learn to challenge the printed word. Similarly, including diverse perspectives in readings can reflect the diversity of backgrounds, interests, and experiences in the group. Sometimes, it is worthwhile to take yet another step and use fiction, poetry, or readings from different sources such as magazines and newspapers. And, whatever readings we choose, we need to be careful to integrate them into the learning activities and discussions.

Chapter Ten

Facilitating Discussion

We read something complex. Perhaps we reread it. We think about it, underline or highlight, write questions in the margin. Then, during a conversation with others, concepts suddenly become clearer. Perhaps another person has just a slightly different way of expressing ideas and what was confusing clicks into place. Or someone may ask a question that clarifies our thinking. There is no denying the value of discussion in learning.

I have a friend and colleague with whom I regularly discuss teaching–his and mine. As we engage in these conversations, we often create a new understanding of what we do and why we do it. We exchange anecdotes about our students and what we do in our classes. I may describe an activity I used in an adult education course; Laurence may then adapt it for use in his short courses on interviewing or résumé writing. I may then adopt his idea, changing it again for another purpose. We sometimes even give each other credit for our own ideas. We lose track of where they originated and who changed what. Through our conversations, we construct knowledge that neither of us could have as easily discovered on his or her own.

Not all knowledge is best acquired through discussion, of course. Learning a new skill, for example, requires repeated practice, and there may not be much to say about it after an initial explanation or demonstration. At this point it would be helpful to review three basic kinds of knowledge (Habermas, 1971) and consider how discussion fits into each before proceeding with guidelines for facilitating discussion. As in all aspects of teaching, we need to be aware of why we are doing what we are doing. In this chapter, I first look at kinds of knowledge, then turn to kinds of discussion, how to set up a discussion, how to monitor it, and finally, how to finish it.

Kinds of Knowledge

Although there are many different ways of classifying knowledge, I find Habermas's system particularly useful in examining teaching and learning. He identifies and describes three different types of knowledge: instrumental, communicative, and emancipatory.

- *Instrumental or technical knowledge* is factual and clear cut. It is cause-and-effect knowledge derived from scientific methodologies.

  > The acquisition of instrumental knowledge is a goal of education in the trades, technologies, and sciences. Although discussion has only a minor role in the area of instrumental knowledge, it should always be included in order to keep learners involved.

- *Communicative knowledge* (called practical knowledge by Habermas) is the understanding of ourselves, others, and the social norms of the community or society in which we live.

It is acquired through language and validated by consensus among people. The acquisition of communicative knowledge is a goal in the study of human relations, political and social systems, and education. Discussion is the primary way we acquire communicative knowledge–we must talk to each other to understand each other.

- *Emancipatory knowledge* is the self-awareness that frees us from constraints.

It is a product of critical reflection and the questioning of beliefs and assumptions. Gaining emancipatory knowledge can be a goal of all learning, as we critically question, for example, the role of technology, which is in itself instrumental knowledge, or the underlying assumptions of a political system, which is in itself communicative knowledge. It is an explicit goal in life-skills learning, literacy programs, self-help groups, women's studies courses, and community action groups. Discussion is essential in order to gain emancipatory knowledge, though it plays a slightly different role here.

Kinds of Discussions

As we know from ordinary social interactions with friends and colleagues, there are many kinds of conversations. We engage in "small talk" about everyday things. We tell anecdotes about others and ourselves. We confide our concerns or problems to someone who helps us deal with them. We discuss political issues. We examine a knotty theoretical issue in conversation with a colleague. Each of these dialogues is very different from the others. So it is in teaching and learning. There is not only one way of having a discussion. I describe four variations here.

- *Informative discussion* is an exchange of information and experiences.

  > Participants contribute what they know to the general pool of information held by the group. They offer information and relate anecdotes from their own professional or personal experience. Each piece of information and each anecdote may bring to others' minds different pieces of information or anecdotes, and as the discussion continues, everyone's understanding of the issue becomes broader and more complex. In my first years of teaching, I thought that talking about experiences was a lower level of discussion and discouraged it. Nevertheless, students persisted in sharing stories, and I now value this kind of discussion.

- *Cooperative discussion* in a group has the goal of solving a problem or completing a task.

  > The group has a common goal and everyone cooperates in order to reach the goal. Students may have a case study to work on, an ethical issue to resolve, or a plan to develop. In cooperative discussion, the end is clear. People want to get the problem solved, the job done. In the workplace, for example, most team learning is of this nature.

- *Collaborative discussion* does not focus on a task or goal, but aims to create new knowledge.

  > This discussion involves the contribution of thoughts, feelings, insights, and ideas. When a colleague and I discuss our teaching, we are not trying to solve a particular problem that either of us faces. We are talking about teaching because we share a passion for our work and enjoy hearing each other's points of view. Through these kinds of exchanges, people construct new knowledge. A group of managers, for example, might gain entirely new insights into

manager-staff relations during a workshop discussion of empowerment.

- *Transformative discussion* critically questions assumptions and challenges perspectives.

> One person presents an argument or position along with supporting evidence or reasons. Others weigh the evidence, examine the reasons, and question the position. This provides an opportunity for participants to look anew at their own assumptions, with the result that they may become more open-minded, clarify what they think, or even revise their opinions. On the other hand, if their arguments are valid, they may maintain their current position.

> The adult education literature refers to this as transformative learning. For example, a health practitioner may subscribe to the traditional medical model, having absorbed that way of thinking from her training and professional community. In a transformative discussion, other participants present alternative positions, such as holistic medicine or wellness models, and question the assumptions underlying the traditional medical model. If the health practitioner sees reasonable alternatives to her point of view during the discussion, she may transform her assumptions and possibly change her practice. If, on the other hand, she still successfully justifies and maintains her original opinion, it is now an examined position.

Setting up a Discussion

Setting up a good discussion requires some practice and lots of intuition. Simply asking people to discuss a topic is usually not enough to stimulate meaningful and provocative comments. However, when participants have experience with discussion and know each other well, less guidance is required.

We always need to clarify the purpose or goal of the discussion, as well as what kind of discussion we hope to facilitate. Participants need to know whether we are planning to engage in informative, cooperative, collaborative, or transformative discussion. However, it is neither necessary nor appropriate to use these labels. Instead we can say, for example, "Let's hear about some experiences you have had with this" to start an informative discussion or "Let's try to see at least two different sides of this issue" to begin a transformative discussion. I recently observed an educator attempting to set up a transformative discussion. Since the students did not understand the goal, they thought that he was merely arguing with them every time they raised a point. They became frustrated and slightly hostile after about 20 minutes of this.

Here are some techniques for eliciting stimulating discussion.

- Set up a structure or framework for a discussion, but be careful, it can act as a constraint as well.

> In the orientation to the master's program in which I am currently teaching, students come in which varied backgrounds. Some people are fairly familiar with adult education practice, but others are not. One of the goals of the orientation is to introduce people to the fundamentals of conducting research in adult education. I need to provide a framework for discussion in this case, as the topics are new to most

people. I use Habermas's three kinds of knowledge (instrumental, communicative, and emancipatory) as a guide. After I explain these terms, the group has a way to talk about how such knowledge could be acquired through research.

- Encourage participants to talk to each other directly rather than to and through the educator.

    If each comment is directed to the teacher, who then responds, and asks for a comment from someone else, a true discussion does not develop. I avoid this by remaining silent and simply not responding to such comments. It may take a minute or two, but another participant will speak if the teacher says nothing. It is also helpful to look away–to avoid eye contact with the person speaking.

- Use discussion questions to help set up a good dialogue.

    Discussion questions can be distributed either in advance of or just before the session. The educator, the participants, or both can prepare the questions. By varying the style of the questions, we can create the kind of discussion we want.

Monitoring Discussion

To maintain a discussion, we need to find a balance between guiding and letting participants be, between supporting and challenging. We need to monitor, that is, to have a sense of the flow of the conversation. We must notice when the talk begins to flag or wander and step in if necessary, at the same time being careful not to interfere automatically or impose our own notion of what should be happening on the group. We need to encourage people to speak by being supportive, but we also need to challenge participants to go beyond their initial observations or thoughts. Finding this balance is not simple. It changes from group to group, and within the same group, it changes from session to session or even hour to hour. Sometimes the absence of a single person from a group can change the whole rhythm of the discussion.

Here I give some general suggestions and guidelines that stem from my experience in leading discussions. Some may be more relevant than others, depending on the context, subject area, students, and preferences of the educator.

- Encourage students to talk to each other rather than only to the teacher.

- Let discussion continue as long as it is lively, interesting, and related to the topic, even if it is not proceeding exactly as anticipated.

- Intervene gently and remind participants of the purpose when the discussion wanders too far from the topic or seems to be changing into a different kind of discussion.

- Ask questions if the discussion only affirms and reinforces when it should be more critical.

  > For example, ask, "How did you come to that view?"
  > or "What evidence did you find to support your
  > position?" or "Why is this important?"

- Be supportive in comments and body language if participants are anxious or timid.

- Redirect the conversation when one or a few individuals do most of the talking.

    Ask such questions as, "What do others think?" or "Can we hear from someone else on this issue?"

- Handle the situation with care if a dominant group member becomes a problem and good discussion ceases.

    A general announcement to the group is never a good idea–the most unlikely individuals may assume that they are at fault. Talk privately to the person or use methods such as a "talking circle"—everyone speaks in turn or a "talking stick"—hand around a baton and only the person holding it speaks.

- Do not interfere if someone is very quiet.

    Ask that person privately if he or she is comfortable. Usually the answer is "yes."

- Listen carefully at all times to the discussion.

    Sometimes, making notes is helpful in order to remember salient points, redirect the talk, return later to important issues, or for a final summary.

Wrapping up Discussion

In a class I observed recently, a lively discussion took place with which the teacher was obviously pleased. However, at a certain point, he clearly wanted to end the talk and go on to another facet of the class. He glanced at his watch in an exaggerated fashion and made several comments about "moving on." Just when I thought he was going to be able to close the discussion, another student made a comment and the conversation started up again. This is a difficult situation, especially when we have worked hard to get the discussion going. It seems wrong to cut it off.

There are only two options here. One is to go with the discussion and abandon the planned agenda; the other is to wrap up the discussion. The first option is fine when we have enough flexibility to do so and do not need to cover material (as did the educator I was observing). On the other hand, there is nothing wrong with ending a discussion. The participants will talk again next time; we are not closing the conversation forever.

There are many different ways to wrap up a discussion. Here I review three basic strategies—summarizing, questioning, and integrating.

- Summarize the discussion to end it in the simplest and most obvious way.

    This means that we need to listen carefully throughout the session and, if necessary, take notes. The summary should be brief (no more than five minutes for a thirty-minute discussion), but it should highlight the main insights and ideas raised by participants. I find it useful to mention those aspects that I personally found interesting. If ideas have come up in the discussion that I have not thought of before, I make sure to say this. Participants are generally very pleased to realize they have contributed to our learning.

- List or review the questions that arose from the discussion.

    Discussions inevitably raise further questions and issues to explore. Pose the questions as ideas to think about between sessions and refer to again the next time the group meets, or raise them as ideas to ponder. Provocative questions encourage people to keep the class or workshop in mind as they go back to the rest of their life.

- Integrate ideas from the discussion into other aspects of the course or workshop.

> Although more difficult to do, this technique can be very useful. In this case, not only highlight the main points, but also talk briefly about the relevance of these points to other concepts. For example, in a class I recently observed, participants were discussing how the Internet is changing our sense of community. People are able to join discussion groups in which individuals are physically located anywhere in the world. But perhaps more importantly, people tend to join discussions in which others share their point of view. The classroom debate had wandered far and wide and some quite radical points were raised. The teacher then skillfully integrated the issues raised in this discussion with other points about our increasing reliance on technology. This kind of wrap-up helps people to keep the larger picture in mind and clarifies the relationships among topics.

- Encourage students to close a discussion themselves by summarizing, questioning, or integrating.

> If people know in advance that they are going to wrap up, they can take notes or prepare questions throughout the discussion.

Summary

Discussion is probably one of the most important learning strategies in adult education. When we are interested in promoting critical thinking or fostering the creation of knowledge through collaboration, discussion is an essential component of our work.

An awareness of Habermas's (1971) three domains of knowledge is useful in determining when discussion is necessary and what kind of discussion is most appropriate. For example, when we are working with instrumental or technical knowledge, discussion plays a lesser role than when we are hoping to bring about communicative or emancipatory learning.

It is important to be aware of the kind of discussion we want to set up. In informative discussion, people exchange experiences and anecdotes. In cooperative discussion, participants contribute what they know in order to solve a problem. In collaborate discussion, people build new group knowledge by integrating their personal knowledge. In transformative discussion, students examine and possibly revise their assumptions. Since these processes are quite different, knowing which one is appropriate helps us to know how to facilitate the discussion.

In setting up a discussion, the purpose should be clear. It is sometimes useful to create a framework or boundaries for the dialogue, although we need to be careful not to let this inhibit creativity and new directions. Discussion questions act as a good guide.

Monitoring a discussion sometimes reminds me of trying to round up the cattle on the farm. Sometimes the cattle all go off in different directions, and you run around the field like a fool. Other times, they all go in one direction and will not stop or change direction. Or, one or two will stubbornly remain behind. There is no surefire way to round up the cattle or monitor a discussion, but I do provide some ideas from my experience.

Discussions can be wrapped up either by the educator or the participants. Summarizing the main points, listing questions arising from the discussion, or integrating the issues into other aspects of the course or workshop are three ways a discussion can be brought to a close.

Chapter Eleven

Getting Feedback on Teaching

In a recent interview, a teacher told me that she had no idea whether or not a class had gone well when she ended the session and left the room. Sometimes, she felt pleased during the class, but afterwards started thinking of all of the things that had gone wrong. Other times, she worried during the actual class, but regarded it more positively later on during the day. This teacher cared deeply about doing a good job. Although she was not a novice teacher, neither was she a senior educator. When I asked her why she did not ask the students what *they* thought of the class, she was surprised. She had never considered anything beyond the standard student questionnaire, which is administered only at the end of a course and therefore does not provide useful feedback while the teaching is going on.

We need frequent feedback to learn. In order to improve continually as teachers, we need to ask for feedback. In many other professions, evaluation of performance is routine procedure, but not in teaching. Except for formal ratings used in promotion, hiring, or renewal decisions, no one tells us how we are doing. In this chapter, I discuss informal feedback, more systematic strategies, and how to use and respond to feedback when we receive it. First, it is important to consider what kind of feedback we want.

What Do We Really Want to Know?

To obtain general feedback, we simply can ask how things are going or what participants would like to see changed. However, when in response people complain about the cafeteria food or just say that everything is fine, such information is not very helpful. When we do not have anything special in mind, asking for general feedback is sufficient. However, if we want reactions to specific aspects of the teaching and learning interaction, we need to ask directly about those aspects. Some aspects of teaching on which we may want feedback include:

- The relevance of the content or objectives to participants' needs and interests.
- The organization of the session or sessions.
- The appropriateness of the methods.
- The difficulty level and clarity of the material.
- The quality of the readings or other resources.
- The usefulness of discussions or group work.
- The degree to which the learning projects or assignments are helpful.
- The participants' comfort level within the group.
- Our relationship or rapport with participants.
- How much people are learning.
- The usefulness of the feedback we give.
- The appropriateness of the grading scheme.
- The quality of the facilities, equipment, or room.

There is no point asking about all of these things at once. The response would probably be perfunctory, as the extent of the questionnaire would overwhelm students. And, even if taken seriously, the resulting feedback itself would be overwhelming, making it impossible to address everything mentioned. Also, it is important to distinguish between those things we can and cannot change. For example, it is useless to ask about the classroom if no other rooms are available.

Informal Feedback Strategies

We acquire feedback informally in many ways when we work with others. For example, as part of a team or committee we perceive how other people regard our contributions through their comments, facial expressions, and body language. In conversation with a friend or family member, we quickly become aware of the hurt feelings, anger, or pleasure in the interaction. This kind of feedback is equally as available to us in teaching and learning interactions as it is in any other relationship with people—if we learn to invite it and pay attention when it is expressed.

- We can ask questions of students; this is one of the simplest ways to obtain feedback.

    > Questions can pertain to the content if we are interested in students' learning, or the process if we want to know about the methods we are using. It only takes a minute to ask, "Is the concept clear?" or "Is this activity helpful?" The more specific the question, the more specific the feedback will be.

- Body language and facial expressions tell us a lot.

> A wealth of information is available to us from observing student behavior. It is best to focus on one individual at a time.

> People who are interested and involved look directly at the person speaking, sometimes leaning forward, and appear to be relaxed and comfortable. Positive reactions to the learning experience also include smiling, nodding, looking attentive, responding verbally, and using hand gestures when speaking.

> People who are uninterested flip through papers, look down or out of the window, glance repeatedly at the clock, or appear tired and bored.

> People who may feel anxious or intimidated tend to blush, make nervous gestures, shrink back, or fold their arms across their bodies.

- We should listen to conversations among participants whenever possible.

> It is important not to eavesdrop, but it can be very helpful to occasionally casually join a group of students and listen to what they say about the content and process. For example, when students are working in small groups or chatting before or after class, join the group to chat and listen.

> When participants are taking in the hallway during a break or coming to or leaving class, this is a good time to ask how things are going. Questions such as, "How did you find that last discussion?" or "What did you think of the reading?" may elicit useful responses. Ask about aspects of the class for which feedback is wanted, but do so in a relaxed, conversational way. Students provide valuable insights in response to such questions.

- I usually invite students to provide feedback by e-mail or voice mail.

If someone is struggling with a reading in the evening or reflecting on a class after it is over, this is the time for her or him to send a quick e-mail. Of course, this process is not anonymous, but if a relationship of trust exists, many people will feel free to share their reactions and comments with the teacher. We must acknowledge the messages by either replying or commenting on them in class.

Systematic Feedback Strategies

Although informal feedback can give us invaluable insights, we should be aware that it sometimes provides a distorted picture. Students may be reluctant to make unflattering or negative comments face-to-face, or one very dissatisfied student's response may loom too large in our minds. Therefore, it is vital to obtain systematic feedback at some point during a course or workshop. The most obvious source of systematic feedback is to survey the participants. In addition, people other than students can offer fresh points of view. I review some of the many different strategies for obtaining feedback here.

- A Quick Check (mentioned in Chapter Three) gives a fast and individual reaction to what has gone on so far.

  > This is my favorite technique for obtaining anonymous feedback from all participants. At the end of a class or partway through a workshop, I hand out blank index cards. I ask people to write on one side of the card what they are enjoying about the session and on the other side what they would like changed. Depending on the context and the feedback I want, I sometimes make these instructions more specific. The

Quick Check takes no more than five minutes and can be used more than once in the same course.

- A brief rating form can give us a good snapshot of what is happening.

    For example, on a scale of 1 to 5, "strongly agree" to "strongly disagree" or YES!, yes, yes & no, no, NO!, have students respond to a short list of statements.

    Examples may include such statements as:

    — So far, this course/workshop is well organized.

    — I am finding the discussions beneficial.

    — So far, I have enjoyed the group activities.

    — The content of this session is relevant to my practice.

    — So far, I am learning a lot.

    The content of the statements should reflect the areas about which we want feedback. Include space for general comments as well. Again, a short form takes only about five minutes to complete.

- We can sometimes read student journals for their reactions to the readings, discussions, or experiences in applied settings.

    A regular check of student journals can provide an excellent source of feedback on teaching, even though this is not their main purpose. However, journals are not anonymous, and if students know we are reading them, they may edit their reactions. Hopefully, a trusting relationship minimizes this.

- Groups of students can be asked to give feedback and then report back to the class.

    In small groups, students can discuss their reactions to a session or particular aspects of a session. A spokesperson then reports for the group, thereby maintaining anonymity for individuals. Alternatively, we can form a student committee with the mandate of collecting comments from all individuals in the group and reporting to the class. Membership on the committee can rotate if this reoccurs over a full term. The comments can be general or specific, depending on what kind of feedback we want.

- Videotape a teaching session for invaluable feedback.

  We can examine what we do in a class or workshop privately and at leisure. A videotape allows us to actually see what we do and become aware of behaviors and mannerisms we may not have known we have. It is helpful to have a set of specific aspects on which to focus. How do I ask questions? Do I speak clearly? What role do I take in discussions? How much do I speak in relation to how much the students speak? Do I create smooth transitions from one part of the session to another? Are my explanations clear? Are my examples useful? Are my summaries concise?

  View the videotape as soon after the session as possible so that it is still fresh, and we can remember what we were thinking or feeling.

  As is the case with all feedback, but even more important to remember here, we need to focus on what we do well, not just on what bothers us. As we continue to learn about teaching, we need to remind ourselves of our strengths.

- It can be helpful to obtain a different perspective by inviting a colleague, friend, or faculty development consultant to observe our teaching.

  The observer need not be familiar with the content— he or she is watching the teaching, but in some circumstances, a person who also knows the subject is more helpful. This person either can observe in a general way, making notes about anything that catches his or her attention or can look for specific aspects of the teaching process. We must inform students why this extra person is present. As with the use of videotape, it is good to discuss the observation as soon as possible after it is complete.

Using Feedback

The result of obtaining feedback on teaching is that we become aware of what we do from a point of view other than our own. Our primary goal is then to sort through the responses and see what we should and/or can do to make changes. However, it is also essential to share and discuss the feedback with participants. To do so shows students that we take their comments seriously; it also gives us the opportunity to ask further questions about their responses. Sometimes, just one person makes a particular suggestion. Rather than make a change based on one or only a few comments, we can ask the group if most agree with the idea. Alternatively, if it seems like a good idea to us, we can try it out and watch how other students respond. Here are a few ideas for sharing feedback.

- Summarize or transcribe students' comments from a Quick Check or rating form and give them back to the group.

  > I sometimes respond to the same questions and include my comments with the summary. In a workshop, written summaries are more difficult to prepare (unless we carry a laptop and printer and find time to type a report while participants are busy elsewhere).

- Use a coffee or lunch break in a short session to have a look at written feedback and make quick tallies of the kinds of comments received.

> For example, we might discover and report that 16 out of 25 people listed the discussions as enjoyable and 4 out of 25 people said the group activities were not useful for them.

- Provide results to all participants through group reports when feedback is elicited in group work.

- Report what we learned to the participants for further discussion after a videotaping or observation.

- Report positive responses received, as well as negative reactions.

   > The focus should not be only on critical comments during any discussion of feedback results with students.

- Review each suggestion for change or identification of potential problem areas with participants.

   > This review gives people a chance to elaborate on what they said and reveals whether most participants agree with any particular change. Sometimes, a person will say, "Oh, it was me who made that comment, and it's not really important." Others will say, "Yes, I didn't write that, but I agree it's something we should think about."

- Discuss any planned changes with participants.

- Indicate which suggestions will not be implemented and why.

Treating feedback as a process to be shared with students in this way makes the process transparent. It demonstrates that we value what students say. Consequently, the next time we ask for feedback, people will be even more thoughtful, careful, and helpful, knowing that we listen, care, and respond.

Summary

I realize that for some teachers receiving feedback is a traumatic experience. I have known people who avoid opening the envelope of student evaluation forms, placing them under a stack of papers for several days before summoning the courage to look at them. At the other extreme, I am so interested in seeing what students have written on the Quick Check cards that I read them the minute I leave the class.

Perhaps teachers dread feedback because they focus solely on the negative comments. Perhaps they do not know what to do with the responses. Perhaps they fear terrible surprises because they have had no ongoing informal feedback to indicate to them how things are going, as was the case with the teacher described at the beginning of this chapter. By asking specific questions, focusing on the positive comments, discussing results with students, and making concrete plans as to how to implement change, I hope that everyone can feel comfortable in obtaining feedback. After all, it is mainly through feedback that we learn more about our practice.

In this chapter, I suggest we think about what it is we want to find out about our teaching before asking for feedback. I suggest several ways of obtaining ongoing informal feedback. In every learning session, we can ask questions of students, observe their body language, invite their comments, and listen to what they are saying. In addition, it is essential to acquire systematic feedback from every participant. Means of accomplishing this are asking for comments on blank cards, giving out a rating form, reading student journals, or having students discuss the learning experience in groups. Sometimes, another perspective altogether is valuable, such as videotaping a class or inviting an observer to comment on our teaching.

Rather than hiding the feedback results from ourselves, we need to review them carefully, discuss them with students, and make practical plans for improvement. Things can only get better when we listen to feedback.

Chapter Twelve

Creating Variety

It was many years ago now, but this moment remains vivid in my memory. I was teaching summer school in the Instructor Development Program in New Brunswick–a program for beginning college instructors. We worked in the "sewing room" in the basement of the building, surrounded by sewing machines and swatches of fabrics, none of which had anything to do with our course. We had decided to spend the first few classes on various facets of group dynamics, so naturally enough, we were working in groups almost exclusively. Over the six-hour classes, we moved from one group activity to another, debriefing and discussing in between. After four or five days of this, the students approached me during a break. "We can't stand one more group thing," they said with a mixture of passion and concern about my possible reaction. I felt just a twinge of resentment; after all, they had asked for these topics. Then, I realized that we had been doing an extraordinary amount of group work and nodded my agreement. The students were primarily tradespeople unused to group work to begin with. What had we been doing? They laughed with relief, and we went back to the classroom to plan a new direction for our work.

There is a point in any course or workshop, usually about one-third of the way through a course or one-half of the way through a workshop, when people feel the need for variety, no matter what they have been doing. Even when I use various strategies much more conscientiously than I did in that sewing-room class, this need always arises. I have learned to prepare for it, even saving a video or an excursion for when a change is needed. In this chapter, I suggest some ways to bring variety into the classroom. I focus on five categories of variety—different people, different media, different settings, different content, and different interactions.

Different People

We may not like to admit it, but our students get tired of each other and us over time. We are not a group of friends who have chosen each other; we are a group of people who share an interest in a subject or a common learning goal. Quite often, we know little else about each other when we first meet. Try some of the following to introduce variety into a course or workshop.

- Change the people who do the teaching.

    In a one-day workshop, this not easy, but having a co-facilitator with whom we alternate sections of the day helps.

- Bring in a good guest speaker, one who has expertise or experience related to a particular topic.

    While the traditional academic or professional guests make valuable contributions, other kinds of guests can be equally effective and perhaps more interesting. For example, in a course on adult development, an older person can talk about her life experiences. In a course on agriculture or environmental issues, a farmer can bring a practical perspective. In a course on early childhood care, a parent and child could be special guests. Graduates of the course or program can relate how they have been able to apply what they learned. Regardless of the course content, we can find creative ways of bringing guests into class.

- Bring a colleague into class or trade classes with a colleague to introduce a fresh perspective on the content, demonstrate a different teaching style, or just add a new face to the group.

> Upon occasion, my group and I have joined the class of a colleague if that group is doing something relevant to our class. The new mixture of people is invigorating for both groups.

- Arrange for student-led sessions to help create variety.

> Although the people remain the same, their roles change. In this case, the educator should participate as a student in the session rather than sit apart, remaining in the teacher role.

> On one occasion, instigated by the participants in our class, everyone brought in a friend, spouse, or family member. Their rationale was that we needed to have "more people" for the exercise planned, but I suspect that they were also looking for change. It was exciting to have so many others in our group for that evening.

Different Media

As I discuss in Chapter Nine, because we tend to rely heavily on readings, an easy way to introduce variety is to use other media.

- Use videos when appropriate.

  Videos are a common and easily accessible choice, available in libraries and, of course, video rental stores. Movies relevant to the course tend to stimulate great interest in any group. When students take responsibility for selecting and acquiring the video, we, too, can sit back and enjoy the show. On a few occasions in my practice, students have selected a video I thought was inappropriate, or a student's choice has offended someone in the group. However, we can make the most of such incidents by using them to stimulate provocative discussion.

- Audiotapes or CDs also can be useful in some settings.

  Playing music during some activities also provides variety.

- Consider using other media such as photographs, paintings, sculptures, or real objects pertaining to a particular topic.

  We need to use our imagination and be as creative as possible in thinking of different media for communication.

- Take advantage of advances in computer technology to provide even more media diversity.

  If the Internet is available in the classroom, it enables us to explore alternative perspectives on any issue. Web-based discussion forums provide a way for students to discuss issues from home—create variety by substituting a web-based discussion for a class. Real-time chat on the computer requires swift typing fingers, but it is an intriguing way of introducing a different medium.

Different Settings

I am not sure why classrooms have to be so uncomfortable. The same tables and chairs and desks appear in every classroom in the country. Adult educators, also, typically work in classrooms that belong to someone else or have a different purpose. We may find ourselves surrounded by mathematics equations, woodworking machines, or pictures of ducks. A change in setting is an excellent way to create variety.

- Set up a field trip or excursion to jog everyone out of the routine of the classroom.

> In some subjects, the choice of field trip locale is obvious, for example, a visit to a hotel for hospitality students, a seniors' home for gerontology students, or an artist's studio for a painting class.
>
> In other disciplines, the choices may be less apparent. We can ask our students for suggestions. By doing this, I have visited a military base (to observe teaching in that setting), a craft school (to see the physical facilities used by crafts teachers), and an outdoor theater (for no real purpose other than to get out of the classroom).
>
> In a group development session, one participant who was familiar with the activity suggested we go to a "ropes course." There we proceeded, under his guidance, to walk around on ropes strung off the ground as a way of building a cohesive and trusting group. We were outside, it was different, and our group did grow closer.

- Move class outside to the lawn or picnic tables for a revitalizing change of venue.

> In my summer school groups, we often do this on a beautiful day.

- Attend a lecture, art show, theatre performance, or concert when relevant to the material.

> If possible, the group can attend such an event instead of class. In evening classes, the times may coincide, but if they do not, as long as all students can participate, it can be a wonderful way to introduce variety into a course.

Different Content

When teachers complain to me that they find the content of their course boring, I wonder why they teach it. "It's the required curriculum," they say, or "The students need to get the basics before we can get into the interesting stuff." Even when there is "material to be covered," we need to keep open the option of making changes in content as a way of creating variety.

Here are three simple and rather obvious ways in which we can make changes in content to perk up a course or workshop.

- First, add a new topic.

> Introduce something stimulating and interesting, perhaps something based on current events or developments in the subject. Especially useful is to ask participants for suggestions. Even only one session on a new topic in a course or 30 minutes in a workshop will go a long way toward energizing everyone.

- Second, discard one or more of the least interesting topics.

    This is where most educators balk. It is difficult to eliminate something that was important enough to include when planning the session. However, a scrupulous scrutiny of the list of topics usually reveals a item or two that can be deleted. Depending on the students and the subject area, it can also be a good idea to ask students what they would prefer to skip.

    Once a topic is dropped, use the time to do something completely different, perhaps a game, a movie, an outing, or just some free time for students to catch up on their readings or learning projects. The change renews people.

- Third, review the plan of the course.

    This is actually a combination of the previous two but it calls for more participant involvement. Stop and say, "It seems that things are not very lively; let's review our course plan." If students were initially responsible for choosing topics, suggesting a review follows naturally from the original planning activity (see Chapter Three). Even if they did not play a part in planning, bringing them into the planning at this point will itself create variety. Ask students to work in groups to review and revise the course plan. If some topics are essential, these are nonnegotiable, but otherwise, giving students as much free rein as possible is ideal.

When I revise the program in this way, I usually provide a fair bit of guidance for students, unless they are experienced at course planning. I suggest that they raise and discuss topics they are interested in and come to consensus on the favorite two, three, or five—the number depends on how many classes are left and how many nonnegotiable topics must remain. They then review current topics and decide which ones to replace with their new choices. The small groups report to the larger group and work out a way to come to agreement. I stay out of it. The result of this is usually a rekindled interest in the course. In a workshop, this is harder to manage, but it can be done. We need to be open to change, prepared with a variety of resources, and willing to put up with some confusion.

Different Interactions

Most adult learning sessions involve a cognitive or a skills-based process. That is, people are learning about ideas, concepts, and issues, or they are learning skills, or some combination of the two. This cognitive or skills-based process largely determines the interactions between teacher and participants. We talk about the content. However, we can introduce variety into the learning environment by including different kinds of interactions.

- Introduce a social event or ritual to change the usual class interaction.

    This can be as ordinary as making tea together. My research methods course is one in which people feel considerable anxiety. "Research" sounds intimidating, and it is a mandatory course in the adult education program. One day in this course, I made a big pot of Tension Tamer tea and brought it into class. This quickly became a ritual. One or two people made tea, others collected cups from the lounge, someone poured, and we passed the cups of hot tea from one person to another around the room. The tension that was relieved by these simple gestures was not a product of the brand of tea.

Other ways of introducing social interaction include having lunch or dinner together, holding class at someone's house, arranging a potluck meal, or bringing snacks into class. There is something about breaking bread together that changes the nature of the relationships in the group.

- Include relaxation or visualization exercises, or build or do something together that is not cognitive in nature to vary the classroom pattern.

In one of my adult education courses, I discovered that one of the participants was a dance teacher. She was delighted to lead us through a short and relaxing dance routine.

A few years ago, two elementary school teachers in one of my summer school courses introduced us to the joys of making a collage by cutting pictures and phrases out of old magazines and gluing them together.

Summary

We often talk about using a variety of methods and materials in adult education, indeed, in education in general. This is the usual solution offered to the problem of accommodating different learning styles. We hardly ever talk about how to create variety in other ways. During that inevitable lull in any course or workshop, those times when people seem to lose interest or run out of energy, we need to think of ways to revitalize the learning environment.

In this chapter, I suggest several ways of creating variety. We can change the people by having guests come in—colleagues or people from the community—or even inviting extra participants. We can change the media by using videos, audiotapes, CDs, or computers. We can change the setting by going on excursions, moving outside, or attending community events. We can make changes in the content by adding or discarding topics or revising the course plan. Finally, we can introduce new kinds of interactions by having tea or a meal together or engaging in some physical activity. Depending on the working and learning context, other ways to introduce variety will occur. We need to experiment, explore, and rely on our learners to help us be creative.

Chapter Thirteen

Being Authentic

Over the past few weeks, I have been engaged in e-mail correspondence with a teacher who insists that authenticity is a spurious concept and my research on authentic teaching a waste of time. "We are all ourselves," he writes, "who else could we be?" As I struggle to respond to his objections, I find myself thinking carefully about what being authentic means. Perhaps if I review how I became intrigued with authenticity, it clarifies the concept. However, unanswered questions remain with me and guide my research.

For me, the importance of understanding authentic teaching grew from two roots. First, I have long been interested in Jung's (1971 [1921]) psychological type theory (see Chapter Five) and how it relates to teaching and learning. It seems clear to me that teachers who have different psychological tendencies have different preferred teaching styles. I am also fascinated by Jung's notion of individuation (see Chapter Twenty), the lifelong process of identifying who we are as distinct from the collective and the community. As we learn who we are, our psychological preferences become clear, natural, and integrated into our way of being.

Second, I have written extensively about transformative learning, the process by which we identify, question, and revise assumptions we had previously absorbed from our community and culture. It seems that transformative learning helps individuation. As we discard those beliefs we had absorbed from others without thought, we become surer of who we are.

When I originally set out to write *Becoming an Authentic Teacher in Higher Education* (Cranton, 2001), the word "authentic" was not even in my mind, let alone in the title. I was going to write about psychological type preferences, individuation, and teaching. My idea was that we need to be ourselves in teaching, in the sense that we go with our personality and preferences rather than trying to be what some other person has decided is indicative of good teaching. It was only when the editor protested strongly (and rightly so) to my proposed title, *No Bad Teachers*, that authenticity came to mind. I was talking about being authentic, being our genuine self, as opposed to playing a role. The literature on how to teach suggests many things. We cannot do all of those things while still following our natural way of being.

My critical correspondent suggests that I am talking about nothing more than competence. I have lots of questions about how good teaching and authentic teaching go together, but I think authenticity is more than competence. In my research, I have observed novice teachers who have not yet attained the polish of their more experienced colleagues, but who are still bringing their genuine sense of self into the classroom. I have also seen expert teachers who appear to be expert actors. If we are to truly relate to students in a way that will foster their growth and development, I do not think we can do this well by acting, though the actor may be quite good at transmitting information in an entertaining fashion.

In this chapter, I review some ways to think about authenticity and bring our genuine self into our practice: the importance of understanding ourselves, knowing what kind teaching suits our nature, telling our teaching story, relating to students authentically, and being authentic within a social context.

Understanding Ourselves

Self-awareness, understanding who we are and why, is a lifelong process. Who we are at 20 can be very different from who we are at 50 or 60 as we go through life's transitions, learn, develop, grow, and experience things. Yet there is also something at the basic core of who we are that seems to remain constant over time. If I think back to who I was at 20, I recognize myself, at the same time as I know that I have changed so very much.

Authenticity is based on a good understanding of ourselves, no matter the life phase we are in. Authenticity exists in youth, middle age, and in our older years. Our understanding matures and deepens with time. Increasing our self-awareness needs to be a deliberate, conscious, continual journey. There is no point where we can say, "Ok, I've got it now. This is me." Increasing our self-awareness can also be a difficult and perhaps painful process—the stuff of counseling and therapy. Here, though, I focus on some fundamental kinds of questions we can ask ourselves in order to deepen our understanding of ourselves with a view to bringing those insights into our teaching.

- What are some words or phrases we use to define who we are?

- How did these descriptors come to be important?

- Do we make judgments based on logic or on values?

- Do we see things as they are or as they could be?

- Are we more outgoing or more inwardly focused?

- What experiences have significantly shaped our lives?

- Why are these experiences significant?

- What are our most cherished values?

- How did these values come to be important?

What Kind of a Teacher am I?

When we consider our personality, values, and experiences, what does this tell us about what kind of a teacher we are? Too many educators spend time trying to be dynamic lecturers when they are naturally quiet people or trying to be extremely well-organized when it is their nature to go with the flow. In Chapter Five, I reviewed psychological type theory in relation to learning style. We can use the same model to understand teaching style (Cranton, 2001).

- The *organized teacher* is one who has a preference for the thinking function.

  > The content of the course is clearly structured, and the relationships among topics are unambiguous. One topic follows logically from another; the sequence of events facilitates understanding the content. Each class has explicit goals or objectives and proceeds in an orderly fashion. Everyone knows what is expected and what is going to happen. Nothing is out of place.

- The *caring teacher* has a preference for the psychological function of feeling.

  > He focuses on participants as people. He establishes a warm and friendly environment in the classroom. He is supportive, has good relationships with students, and considers the needs and interests of everyone in the group. The caring teacher genuinely listens and cares, going out of his way to do things to make people comfortable and to avoid conflict. Everyone feels well looked after and safe.

- The *practical teacher* prefers the sensing function.

  > She enjoys encouraging experiential learning, learning by doing. She is realistic and down-to-earth. She brings real objects into the classroom and takes students on field trips. Her students work with real-life problems. The relevance of the content to students' lives or future career is clear. The practical teacher uses a lot of examples and illustrations. Everyone sees how the material can be applied.

- The *creative teacher* prefers to use his intuitive function.

  > He sees teaching as an opportunity to help people and things change and improve. He is enthusiastic about visions of the future, both personal and professional. He inspires participants to share his vision and engage in new and exciting learning. He experiments with his

teaching, rarely doing something the same way twice. Everyone is carried along with this teacher's innovative way of seeing the subject area.

Few people fall clearly into these categories; in fact, these categories border on stereotypes. What we can do is use such descriptions as anchor points to determine our teaching preferences. Are we more like the organized teacher or more like the caring teacher or somewhere in between, and if so, what features do we share with each? It is especially important to reflect on the kind of teacher we are by nature, not the kind of teacher we would like to be or think we should be. Authenticity comes from an understanding of who we are and how we bring those qualities into our work with students.

Telling Our Teaching Story

In my adult education courses, students often choose to write an educational autobiography–their teaching story. They sometimes present their story to the group in order to hear others' comments and questions. They find telling this story to be extremely helpful in learning who they are as teachers. It enables them to relate personal experiences to their teaching and find a deeper meaning in teaching anecdotes. For example, when I asked one of the participants in my research project on authentic teaching to talk about how she came to be a teacher, she started with a story about taking her younger siblings on walks and helping them identify plants when she was a child. She saw herself as a teacher during these walks, although it was many years before she "accidentally" started teaching botany.

It is important to actually tell or write our story, not just think about it. It is in the telling, especially when other people read or listen, that we seem to make the connections that help us understand what being a teacher means to us. We need to learn which things about teaching really matter to us and which things we have picked up from others. Here I provide some questions, which can be used as a guide to telling our teaching story. Not all questions will be relevant to all teachers, and there may well be questions that are important to some individuals that I have missed (adapted from Cranton, 2001).

- What is our earliest memory of teaching?

- What did we think of teachers or teaching as a child?

- How did people in our community view teachers?

- Did we deliberately choose to teach or fall into it?

- Are there teachers in our family? Amongst our friends?

- What teachers do we admire?

- What facets of our basic nature are parts of what teachers do?

- What qualities do most teachers have that we do not have? How are we different from other teachers?

- Which personal qualities do we not take into the classroom?

- What was our first teaching experience like?

- How has our teaching changed? Why has it changed?

In telling our teaching story, it is particularly helpful to consider what characteristics we bring into teaching naturally. Do we enjoy helping others? Explaining things? Do we want to improve the world? It is equally helpful to reflect on how we are different from the collective concept of teacher.

Relating with Students

Teaching is a specialized form of communication that has learning as its goal. Good communication relies on an understanding both of ourselves and of the person with whom we are communicating. The better the relationship between the people, the more meaningful the communication. In trying to understand how authentic teaching relies on relating with students, I often think of a quote from Hollis (1998, p. 13). He writes, "the quality of all our relationships is a direct function of our relationship to ourselves," and "the best thing we can do for our relationships with others...is to render our relationship to ourselves more conscious." In other words, the more we understand ourselves, the better we can relate to others.

Jarvis (1992, p. 113) takes this one step further when he writes, "Authentic action is to be found when individuals freely act in such a way that they try to foster the growth and development of each other's being." It is through our relationship with students that we engage in authentic teaching.

As we become conscious of who we are as teachers and people, we become conscious of how we relate to our students. What do we do or say to establish relationships? Which students do we particularly like? Why? Which students do we dislike or resent? Who annoys us? Why? How do we behave toward students we dislike? Do we spend time outside of class with students? How much do we learn about their personal lives? In Chapter Six, I provide some suggestions about how to establish different kinds of relationships with students–relationships that suit our natural inclinations and are therefore more likely to be authentic.

Authenticity in a Social Context

There are at least three levels of social context which influence how we are or can be authentic: the institution or organization where we work, the community within which we live, and the larger society of which we are a part. We need to come to an understanding of the values and norms regarding teaching and learning at each of these levels so that we can determine how our own values and beliefs are congruent with or at odds with our social context. Such an understanding allows us to be ourselves instead of getting swept along with the majority.

> When I think of institutional values, the experience of my friend Laurence immediately comes to mind. Laurence repeatedly teaches a one-week course on résumé writing. No matter how many times he teaches this course, it is different each time as the learners are different each time. However, the institution wants to "can" the courses, to prepare standardized packages which everyone will follow. This comes into direct conflict with Laurence's values, and he would leave the position should he be forced to teach this way.

This is the kind of thing we need to think about at all levels of our social context in order to maintain our authenticity. Here, I suggest some questions to guide that thinking.

- How do our colleagues talk about teaching?

- What are the administrative expectations regarding teaching?

- Is there anyone in the institution or organization who will or can tell us how to teach?

- What is the mission statement of the institution?

- What kind of support is there for learning about teaching?

- How is teaching evaluated?

- In our community, how are teachers regarded?

- Is there community interest in adult education?

- Are there expectations in the community as to what educators should do?

- How is adult education portrayed in the media?

- In the larger society, what are government views on adult education? What funding and support is there?

- Do people in our society value education?

- Is there a collective idea of what a teacher should be like?

We need to reflect on where we stand in relation to the social norms we identify. Where our beliefs and values are different from those held in the larger context where we work, we should think about where and if we can compromise and what the consequences of not compromising might be.

Summary

Authenticity is an elusive concept. The more I struggle to understand it, the more slippery it seems to become. I do believe that being authentic is integral to being a good teacher and helping learners grow and develop. If we speak through a mask, play a role, or envelop ourselves in a persona, we cannot form the kind of relationship we need in order to communicate well with students.

A part of being authentic is coming to understand ourselves–our values, beliefs, and preferences. We need to examine our experiences and see how they have shaped who we are. This personal knowledge helps us to understand what kind of a teacher we naturally are and prevents us from trying to be the kind of teacher other people think we should be. One way of knowing who we are as a teacher is to tell our teaching story. How did we become a teacher and what does it mean to us?

Relationships are central to teaching, and authenticity is central to relationships. We need to be cognizant of how we relate to our students and bring our sense of self into that relationship.

Although it often seems that our classrooms are isolated from the rest of the world, we do work in a multi-leveled social context. We are influenced by that context whether we are fully aware of it or not. In order to establish where we stand in relation to the social norms that surround us, we need to reflect on what those norms are and how we fit in or not. Running with the herd is not authentic.

Chapter Fourteen

Using Group Work

Whenever I observe educators talking to overhead transparencies, chalkboards, or PowerPoint slides while students sit passively, I wonder why these teachers do not encourage more interaction with and among students. The topics are interesting; the lectures contain provocative ideas for debate. Finally, after 45 minutes or more of watching and listening have gone by, the teachers often ask students if they have any comments. Perhaps the students have become too accustomed to receiving information to be able to rouse themselves to speak. Comments are rare.

On the other hand, this reaction of mine may indicate only that I expect others to teach just as I do. I must always question myself carefully, talk to other teachers, decide when and why group interaction is appropriate, and never prescribe one style over another.

It was over 25 years ago that I first tried group work with a class, but I still remember it clearly. I was a new teacher, young, and very nervous about what I saw as letting go and losing control of the class. The course was on research methods in education; the students were counselors who had little interest in the subject. It was a required course. I knew the content well and found it interesting myself, but my youthful enthusiasm only seemed to make things worse. The counselors resented me, I am sure. I no longer remember the specific topic, but one day in desperation, I suggested that people work together in small groups to solve a research problem. Counselors like people. They like to work together. The room changed. It became alive. I learned something very important about teaching.

In this chapter, I first discuss how to deal with some problems inherent in group work and review three kinds of groups. I review what we can hope to accomplish through group work. I then turn to some practical considerations in order to create good, effective groups. How should groups be formed? What stages do groups go through if they stay together over time? How should the room be set up? What direction is needed? And finally, how do we bring the small groups back together into the larger group?

Problems in Group Work

As I mention in Chapter Twelve, I certainly have been guilty of overusing group work. While it is pleasant to see people working together, talking, and enjoying themselves, some problems can surface.

When group work is used as a learning activity in a class or workshop, and not as a graded project, it is fairly easy to address the small problems that might arise. If students in a group do not get along, or if one person dominates the discussion, we can rearrange the group's membership the next time around. If people struggle with how to work together effectively, we can take some time to discuss group dynamics and the skills required to work in groups. It might be helpful, for example, to have group members take on various roles such as recording, leading, summarizing, and reporting.

When group work is graded, other kinds of issues may arise. A group receiving a common grade may lead to concerns about equitable contributions to the project, for example. Such issues are more likely to arise in contexts where the learners are not skilled at group work or where there is a noticeable variation in experience and knowledge among the group members. It is useful, in these circumstances, to have individual group members record and report on their contributions to the project. When self-evaluation is used or when there are no grades, as is often the case in adult education, such issues disappear.

Kinds of Groups

In Chapter Ten, I refer to cooperative, collaborative, and transformative discussions. This same framework is useful in considering the different purposes of group work.

- Cooperative group work is appropriate if we want students to solve practical problems in any subject.

> People contribute their knowledge and experience to solving the problem; the combined efforts of a group are more likely to lead to good solutions than the effort of one individual. The success of this relies, of

course on the maturity, experience, and expertise of the individual group members.

The process is one in which students learn and benefit from each other's areas of expertise. "Problems" to be solved can include case studies, tasks, building projects, laboratory work, research projects, or any learning activity in which there is a product or solution.

- Collaborative group work is appropriate when the goal is to create something, construct a new way of viewing an issue, develop alternative plans or models, or design systems.

Students bring together their ideas, values, beliefs, experiences, knowledge, and preferences to make something new. This type of group work differs from the previous problem-solving variety in that any number of valid outcomes is possible.

For example, students may work together to write a play, design a plan to foster staff communication, create a process to involve the public in forestry management, or develop a workshop on learning styles. Any of these activities will lead in different directions, depending on the ideas of the participants.

- Transformative group work is appropriate when the goal is to lead participants to question and reflect on their assumptions, beliefs, and perspectives.

In a class I attended recently, the educator was working with a group of participants whose perspective on how to manage forests was objective and scientific. The teacher hoped to encourage them to consider as well wider social values, such as the impact of forests on communities and people and the spiritual dimension of a forest. What he was trying to create was a process in which students would question their opinions and begin to consider alternatives. Participants help each other articulate and question the assumptions and values of the position they hold.

Whenever it is relevant and meaningful to question an accepted practice, the status quo, the system we work in, the way we think about groups of people, how and why we do things as we do, political practices, or media portrayals of issues, group work is extremely useful. Participants both challenge and question each other, and respond and reflect ideas in a way that helps them clarify for each other the assumptions underlying what they think.

In addition to identifying the kind of learning we hope to achieve through group work, another decision we face is whether group work should be used regularly throughout a course or workshop or only at certain points. This depends on the rhythm and flow of the learning session.

- We should schedule group work later in the session if our plan involves first imparting information with students then reacting or working with the material.

- At other times, it works best when participants first share their experience and knowledge through group work and then proceed from there.

- On still other occasions, we may schedule a group activity that supports each of the topics included.

What Else is Accomplished through Group Work?

- Group work helps maintain student interest and motivation.

As noted earlier, listening to one person speak over an extended period of time is trying, no matter how much we like the subject. With the possible exception of some outstanding motivational speakers, focusing constant attention on one person is difficult. When we read, we can put the book down and do something else for a few minutes or stop and think about a point. However, when someone is speaking to us, we are forced to keep up with his or her pace. Group work helps to break this up.

- Group work also serves to provide social support for individuals, to relieve stress and anxiety, and to promote self-esteem.

We need to feel that we belong and are appreciated by others. Often, adult learners returning to school have a particularly strong need for acceptance and support. They worry that they have forgotten how to study, that they are out of date, that they have nothing of interest to say. A good group experience helps people realize that others value their contributions as well as them as people. Our social and psychological development takes place through interactions with others.

- We still need to vary our methods, as some students do not enjoy group work.

Some students may be impatient with less able peers and feel that their time is being wasted. We need to keep this in mind and be sure to include a variety of strategies (see Chapter Twelve).

Forming Groups

There are several different ways of forming groups. Sometimes, how we do this does not matter, but on other occasions, it is important to plan.

- We should group people together who have similar work experiences when, for example, the group work is designed to focus on work-related matters.

- When we want participants to challenge each other's views, it is time to arrange for people with different backgrounds to work together.

- Groups can be formed randomly to avoid the tendency of students to always sit with the same people.

    > One way to do this is to decide how many groups are wanted, say five groups of four people. Now go around the room with each person saying a number in turn—one, two, three, four, and over again, one, two, three, four until all have spoken. All of the people who said "one" become a group, as do all the people who said "two" and so on. This technique ensures that the groups are randomly formed.

- We can also ask the participants to form groups in any way they wish.

    > In this case, it is most likely that those people who know each other or who have something in common will join forces. At the beginning of a course or workshop, this may be the best strategy as it gives people a sense of comfort to be able to work with those whom they know.

- Sometimes homogenous groups add a different meaning to the process.

    > Shared interests, work experiences, background, or learning style can be the basis for selection. If we know enough about our students, we can suggest the groupings, or we can say, "everyone who has some experience with online learning should join this group" (or whatever the relevant characteristic might be).

If we want to group people based on similar learning styles, we may need to find a way to assess learning style (see Chapter Five) unless it has already been done.

Homogenous groups have the advantage of making participants feel comfortable and safe, but the disadvantage is not bringing a variety of views to the table. The choice depends on our purpose in using group work.

- Deliberately mixed or heterogeneous groups are equally valuable in other contexts.

We may, for example, want mixed learning style groups. In each group there would be individuals with preferences for thinking, feeling, sensing, and intuition. Or, we may want groups where people from different work contexts are represented (the corporate world, government, colleges, and so forth). Heterogeneous groups allow people to bring their various strengths and experiences into the process.

- Generally, we should use different ways of forming groups at different times.

It is especially important not to use homogeneous groups over an extended period. Students need to hear other perspectives, whatever the content or issues may be.

Stages of Group Development

If small groups stay together over an extended period, say working together on a research project or constructing a complex design, the group will change over that time. It is useful to be aware of this process of development so as not to panic when conflict arises. There are different ways of talking about group development in the literature, but Tuckman's (1965) model has withstood the test of time. It has probably survived because of its simplicity and the vivid images conjured up by the labels Tuckman used: *forming, storming, norming, performing,* and *adjourning.*

- In the *forming* stage, group members get to know each other.

    Individuals acquire basic information about each other and becoming familiar with each other's personalities and preferences.

- In the *storming* stage, people come into conflict.

    The differences people initially found interesting begin to annoy them. Arguments arise; some groups cannot survive this stage, especially if there are fundamental discrepancies in values and beliefs.

- The third stage, *norming,* finds the group learning to work with each other.

    Group norms, what is acceptable and what is not, are established. People take on certain roles to keep the group functioning.

- In the *performing* stage, participants work together effectively and efficiently.

    They complete the task, solve the problem, create new knowledge, or help each other question their beliefs and assumptions.

- When the group work ends, the group *adjourns,* and people say good-bye.

    It is important to allow time and space for this to occur. It is helpful to hold closing discussions, review the learning that has taken place, and sometimes to make plans as to how and when the group may meet again.

Physical Considerations

Although the characteristics of the room in which we work may seem of minor importance, they actually can have a profound influence on the quality of group work. Rooms where chairs are fixed to the floor or the desks are in tiers, arranged for a lecture, make group work difficult (but not impossible). A crowded room or one that is too small can become exceedingly noisy when people are working in groups.

- We should do our best to avoid a room with fixed chairs or tiers of chairs when planning group work.

    > If another location is not available, participants will have to turn in their chairs to form groups.

- "Break-out" rooms are ideal, smaller rooms near the main room to which participants can move to work in groups.

- If only one room is available, it is best if the whole group is small enough and the room is big enough to allow space between the smaller working groups. Ideally, the acoustics of the room allow the sound to be absorbed rather than echoed.

    > When we are working in one room, we should consider whether tables and chairs should be arranged in groups prior to starting or not. Doing so saves time initially, but makes it harder to change from one activity to another.

- If the initial seating arrangement is a circle or horseshoe, then tables and chairs will need to be moved each time a group activity takes place.

    > This takes time and is noisy, but it allows for more flexibility in forming groups.

Giving Directions

We have probably all experienced the uncertainty of being placed in a group at a workshop or seminar and wondering what are we supposed to be doing in that group. If directions are vague, or given quickly and only verbally by the facilitator, the group work is off to a bad start.

I give written group-work directions on a handout for students to take with them to wherever their group is meeting. I usually prepare this handout in point form. For example, the direction sheet might look like this.

Adult Development Case: Group Activity

Goal: To apply Sheehy's model to our own experiences and a case study.

1. Form groups with four or five individuals in each.

2. In your group, first explore your reactions to the reading from Gaily Sheehy's book. What did you like or not like and why? Does her model reflect your own experiences?

3. Now, think of yourselves as a group of counselors who are meeting to discuss the case of Walter and Evie. *[The case study could be on a separate sheet, or included here.]* What would you advise Walter and Evie to do? Try to come up with three or four concrete suggestions, taking into account the points raised in our reading.

4. In the larger group, some suggestions from each small group will be presented.

The directions are clear, yet they leave room for flexibility and a variety of responses. This constitutes a collaborative learning activity, one in which many possible actions could be taken.

Some educators like to include a time frame in their directions. I tend not to do this (see Chapter Eight), but if doing so, it should be included it in the direction sheet.

Reporting Back

It is important to plan for some kind of reporting from groups after group work finishes. Participants are usually proud of their contribution and want to share it with others. In addition, such reporting can act as a stimulus for a good large-group discussion, if the topic is continued. There are several ways to conduct reporting.

- All groups report.

    In this case, each group gives a brief summary of what they discussed and responds to questions and comments from other groups. This option takes the most time.

- Each group reports only on what they said that differs from the previous group reports.

    Be sure to change around the order of presentation, so that each group has a chance to be first.

- Each group gives just one example of what they explored or decided.

- Only some of the groups report in any one session.

    If the class is very large and has broken into many small groups, this is an option. If a missed group feels an urgent need to share their responses, they will usually tell us.

Summary

Group work can be used in most courses and workshops and in most subjects, although the nature of the task will vary from one setting to another. When students are solving problems, creating new knowledge, or transforming existing perspectives, group work can facilitate the learning process. As well as being a generally effective learning strategy, group work motivates students, provides social support, validates people, and bolsters self-esteem.

Groups can be formed randomly, students can choose with whom to work, or group structure can be homogeneous or heterogeneous, based on a relevant characteristic. There are advantages to each way of forming groups; how we do this should vary from one occasion to another.

If small groups stay together for an extended period, they go through some fairly predictable stages of development: forming, storming, norming, performing, and, in the end, adjourning. To facilitate group work, it is helpful to be aware of and prepared for such stages.

Some things we may not consider important can influence how well groups work, for example, the nature of the room and the kind of directions given to groups. And finally, it is important to give groups the opportunity to share the results of their work with others.

Chapter Fifteen

Designing Learning Activities

By learning activity, I mean anything students engage in, inside or outside of the classroom, individually or with others, to further and to apply their learning. I am especially interested in those activities with the potential to encourage people to question and be critical of their own and society's assumptions and values, including the assumptions inherent in the discipline. I still remember "learning activities" from my early school days, where, given very definite guidelines, we made something or colored something so that every child produced the same product at the end. You could not tell one Halloween pumpkin from the next. This is not the kind of activity I am interested in here, though there is good reason to learn to do something before we learn to question it. But in adult education, our goal is more often to transform rather than form. Even when we are forming new knowledge, as adults, this process is likely to rub up against something we already knew and alter it. Perhaps it is like a spider web. Children build a spider web of new knowledge. Later, if we add a new piece or remove an old piece of the web, it has consequences for the whole structure.

In this chapter, I review a variety of learning activities, and for each, I emphasize how the activity can be used to encourage people to think, question, reflect, and become more open to alternative points of view. Although I have grouped the activities according to whether they are most appropriate for a class or workshop or outside of class, the line between these categories blurs at times.

In-Class and Workshop Activities

- In a *role play*, participants work with a scenario, realistic or fanciful, and a cast of characters. They improvise dialogue and action to enact what might happen in the situation.

  > For example, participants can act out a manager-staff meeting in which the goal is to resolve conflict in the workplace, or they might dramatize a scene in which customers are upset with service in a restaurant, hotel, or shop. During a more imaginative enactment, people may take on roles as different parts of a software program or cells in the body. By acting something out, students bring a situation or idea to life and are able to see it much more vividly than if they simply read or talk about it. In addition, role-plays take place in the safety of the classroom—there are no actual angry customers in the classroom.

- In order to facilitate critical thinking in a role play, participants can take on different rather than familiar roles.

  > This helps people question and possibly shift their habitual point of view. For example, in a workshop for managers, people can become staff members temporarily and see their side of the picture. Another way to encourage different points of view is to change the roles around so that everyone plays another part. Those that do not participate can observe and help with the discussion afterwards. When people are very

uncomfortable with role playing, we should not insist they join in.

- *Debates* are formalized discussions in which teams of people argue for or against a particular point of view.

> While formal debates include time limits, rebuttals, and a moderator, a more flexible approach is also effective. The choice of structure will depend on how comfortable students are with debating. For example, just dividing the group in half and having the members debate two sides of an issue, with someone to chair the session, can be as effective as the more formal style. The issue chosen should be controversial, one on which people have or can assume different opinions.

- To encourage people to engage in alternative ways of thinking, try the critical debate format.

> In this case, individuals argue for a position opposite to the one they hold. Although this format initially seems contrived and uncomfortable, it almost inevitably produces good insights. I have seen people completely change their minds about an issue because of a critical debate. Last term, we conducted a debate on a local issue of whether or not there should be tolls on the major highway going through New Brunswick. Two participants, each debating on opposite sides and against their own views, argued themselves into the other position much to their amazement.

- The traditional *case study* method comes from the study of law and business, but now is used in almost any subject.

> It consists of a real-life, or at least realistic, problem, including all of the characters, the background of the problem, and the events that have led up to the problem. Case studies may vary from a paragraph or two to several pages in length. They should be

challenging and thought provoking, and have no obvious answer. A case study ends with a question or a series of questions about what people in the situation should do next. It is ideal if participants can identify with the people in the case study or relate it to their own experiences, either professional or personal.

Individuals, pairs, small groups, or all participants can work on case studies. I usually find it is a better learning experience if people work collaboratively. The discussion that follows the case study should highlight differences among the solutions generated and encourage questioning of the assumptions underlying those solutions. That is, if participants say that the manager needs to learn to communicate more effectively with her staff, in the discussion we should question what that means, how it may come about, and why it is important.

- *Critical incidents* were originally developed as a means of collecting research data but have been adapted for use in the classroom (Brookfield, 1995).

    Students are asked to think back over the last six months or year of their professional or personal lives and recall an incident, positive or negative (or sometimes both), that occurred in a specified context. For example, I might ask people to think of their worst experience related to evaluating student learning or to recall their best ever class. Participants then describe this incident in writing. I provide guiding questions, such as, "Who was involved in the incident?" "Where did it happen?" "What insights did you gain from it?" The power of the critical incident is that it draws on students' own experiences rather than someone else's, as in the case study.

    The incidents are then discussed in pairs, small groups, or the whole group if it is not too large and if people are comfortable with each other. During the discussion, participants ask critical questions of each other. Critical questions (see Chapter Eighteen) are those in which we question how and why people came to hold a point of view. For example, participants might ask, "How did this come about?" "Why did you handle it this way?" "What values do you think your action is based on?" It should be clear that there are no right answers. The purpose of the activity is to help people articulate and question their assumptions.

- A *simulation* is a situation in which some facets of reality are present, but students are still working in a safe environment.

> Computer simulations, for example, have been around for decades. Simulations may involve designing bridges, diagnosing patients, or growing plants. I have worked on a computer simulation for disabled students who were learning to recognize and follow street signals. The students acquired the basic information needed for navigating the streets without putting themselves in real danger. In the classroom, students can simulate parliamentary procedures, nursing home care, or conducting a research project.
>
> Simulations further removed from participants' experiences can also be designed with the specific goal of eliciting values. A common generic format is one in which there is some crisis in which, for example, people are at sea in a sinking boat or washed up on a desert island or in a radiation-free room following a nuclear explosion. The cast of characters then may include a teacher, child, nurse, priest, and so on. Sometimes objects are included—perhaps ropes, matches, or oars. Decisions include how to survive, how to escape, or who to leave behind, as room exists only for a certain number of people.
>
> In the discussion that accompanies the decision-making, participants become aware of their assumptions and values. In order for simulations to

encourage critical thinking about values and issues, the discussion following the event needs to examine the reasons for the choices made. Why save the nurse rather than the teacher? Why attempt to escape rather than wait for help?

- *Games* are abstract representations of reality and usually have an element of competition and a winner.

> Games are used in education to help learners apply what they have learned. I have also seen games that foster a more critically reflective process. For example, students in my classes have developed board or card games in which players progress through developmental stages, tell anecdotes from their own lives, and question each other statements. It takes some time and imagination, but we can develop (or perhaps find) games suited to our subject area that encourage introspection and reflection.

- *Laboratories* are commonly found not only in the sciences, but also in many other contexts, such as second language learning, psychology, early childhood education, computer studies, some trades, and even reading.

> A laboratory is a setting where people learn to do something in a controlled and safe environment. It is more realistic than a simulation as only the physical environment is not natural, every other aspect is real. Laboratories have as their main purpose the application of knowledge in a protected place. Sometimes, though, laboratory activities go beyond this. When students have the opportunity to question, create, develop their own innovative projects, and collaborate to generate new knowledge in a laboratory environment, we are able to stimulate critical thinking.

Outside of Class

- *Fieldwork* is a learning activity in which students perform under supervision in natural settings outside of the classroom.

  > This process emphasizes the application of classroom learning in real settings and serves to increase participants' independence, responsibility, and self-direction.

  > Fieldwork takes a variety of forms. Students working individually or in teams outside of the classroom can independently engage in fieldwork activities. Group activities may be integrated within a course. An entire course may take place in the field.

  > In a variation of fieldwork, *service learning*, students take positions in organizations, usually as volunteers, to learn more about their area of study.

  > When we arrange fieldwork for our students or send them out independently, we must ensure that the situation is in the field is adequate. It is important that students have a good learning experience and not be relegated to sweeping floors or be frustrated by uncooperative staff. To this end, we need to visit the setting and establish ground rules with the staff and managers.It is also important that participants are clear about what they are doing in the field. Goals can be quite open and flexible, but goals should be specified. Ideally, we have the opportunity to meet with students regularly during their fieldwork and raise reflective and critical questions. This happens naturally, of course, if we take students on a field trip as a part of a course, but if students are out of the classroom for extended periods, meetings should be arranged.

- Written work, particularly *essays* or *papers,* are among the most common out-of-class learning activities in adult and higher education.

Davis (1993) recommends that less-experienced students be given clear, realistic, well-defined topics, along with a handout of guidelines, and that in some cases the writing assignment should be broken down into parts. For example, students may hand in an outline for comments, then a first draft, and finally the completed essay. Such a process will certainly help those people who are new to writing essays or anxious about the process. On the other hand, when people have a chance to flounder and splash around while we support their efforts, the learning may be more meaningful.

When learners are more experienced, or even with less experienced but confident people, there is great value in individuals choosing topics based on their interests and needs.

Students should always be encouraged to go beyond summarizing and paraphrasing what other people have written. As part of learning to think about subjects for themselves, people should incorporate their own views and experiences and carefully analyze the points of view they encounter. That we expect students to do this should be made clear. Our comments on their work should include support for their critiques, as well as questions to challenge their thinking.

- I particularly like to see participants use *journals* as an out-of-class learning activity (see Chapter Two).

Although there are many different journal formats suggested in the literature, I prefer to leave the style and format of a journal completely up to the writer. The only thing I suggest is that people do not simply report on what has happened, but that they include their own thoughts, feelings, and observations related to anything we are discussing or doing in class. People may hesitate initially, and if they do, I suggest they try an entry or two and then give it to me to comment on.

This is usually enough to break through the beginner's insecurities.

Journals provide a wonderful medium for people to reflect on their learning, expand their understanding of readings or other activities, integrate ideas, and express their feelings. Regardless of whether the educator or a classmate reads the journal, or even if the journal remains private, learners express considerable satisfaction with this as an activity. I should note, though, that I never require people to keep journals, and there are those who choose not to do so.

- There are many other *alternative writing activities* learners can engage in.

Sometimes, rather than writing an abstract paper or keeping a lengthy journal, it is appropriate for students to write letters, biographies, autobiographies, book or article reviews, poems, reports on interviews, or reports on other out-of-class activities. We can be as imaginative in such assignments as we like, or better yet, we can encourage participants to use their ingenuity in coming up with writing ideas.

Examples of letters include a letter to a famous person from history, a letter written from the perspective of another person, a letter to the editor of the newspaper, or a letter written to a younger version of ourselves.

Biographies or autobiographies, especially if written in a story format, are an interesting way to explore our own and others' ideas, experiences, and feelings.

A book review resembles a paper or essay if written in a formal style but can be done less formally. Recently, in my adult development course, a student wrote a review of Margaret Laurence's *Stone Angel* in which she described people from her own life whom she saw as parallel to the characters in the novel. This mix of autobiography and book review led the student to insights into both her own life and the lives of the people in the novel.

Poetry is a wonderful outlet for those who like to write poetry. The ideas and feelings that can be expressed in this genre are difficult to do in an essay or paper.

If people conduct an interview outside of class, or visit a site to observe a specific activity or process, they can write a report or, less formally, a description of what they did. As always, we are encouraging students to use the writing process to explore different ways of thinking about things.

- There are a variety of other *creative learning projects*, aside from writing, in which students can depict what they are learning and what it means to them.

I encourage students to consider expressing themselves through drawing, painting, sculpture, crafts, music, photography, film, or drama. Some individuals who do not consider themselves artistic may choose such an option as a way to explore another side of themselves (see Chapter Three). Others enjoy the opportunity to work in a medium with which they are comfortable.

It is probably best not to put too many parameters on creative projects, other than that they should be related in some way to the learning experience in the course. Not every educator will be comfortable with students engaging in such activities, but I would encourage anyone to experiment with this idea, even if in a limited fashion. The products can be remarkable.

Summary

New educators and even those of us with more experience often struggle to come up with interesting learning activities, either for use in class or for projects outside of class. In this chapter, I hope I have provided some idea of the variety of things our learners can do. I have focused on those kinds of activities which, in my experience, encourage people to question, reflect, and think in a different way.

Most activities should have a well-defined purpose and be discussed after their completion. Nevertheless, there are occasions when it is important to let things flow in the direction they go. The more comfortable we become in using innovative learning activities, the more we feel able to encourage spontaneity and unusual paths. The extent to which a teacher does this has to be his or her individual decision.

Role plays, debates, case studies, critical incidents, simulations, and games all provide a venue for seeing issues from a different point of view and having fun while doing so. The laboratory environment, though most often used to give students the opportunity to apply theoretical knowledge, can also become a setting for critical thought.

Fieldwork gives us a wonderful opportunity to encourage learners' independence and self-direction. There are many ways, ranging from the informal, impromptu adventure to the more formal service learning in which fieldwork can be incorporated into adults' learning experiences.

The most commonly used out-of-class learning activity is the essay or term paper. But there are other good ways of using writing as a way of learning. Journals allow students to incorporate their personal reflections and feelings into their writing. Letters, biographies, autobiographies, reviews, poems, and reports are all alternative writing assignments. If students are encouraged to write from different perspectives, critical thinking is encouraged. Finally, although I recognize this is not to everyone's taste, creative learning projects are worth considering. I know that I remember the quilts, sculptures, and paintings long after I have forgotten the arguments made in the best of essays, and I suspect the learners do too.

Chapter Sixteen

Challenging and Supporting

Yesterday, I observed an educator who seemed to possess a magic balance of challenge and support in his teaching. He asked the penetrating question that took the student's thinking one step further. He settled back with friendly eyes and a smile, listening to another student speak. He suddenly leaned forward and asked, for example, "Why do you say that?" or "How could that be achieved, if what you say is true?" He included statements such as, "That's a very valid point; I agree, and in my experience, it also goes like this..." I took notes, trying to capture the way he came into and went out of the discussion, encouraging and supporting, yet also pushing and challenging, and finding the best moment to do each.

I envied the ease with which this teacher achieved such a good balance. It is not an easy thing to do. He had a small class. The students were working at an advanced graduate level, and they obviously knew each other and their teacher very well. They were working in a comfortable room with sofas and soft chairs. These things help, but they do not make up the whole picture. Personally, I find achieving a balance between supporting and challenging students to be one of the most difficult aspects of my teaching. I have a tendency to favor support over challenge; challenge sometimes feels uncomfortable for me, and I need to make the effort to think deliberately about when to press learners into a more critical stance.

In Chapter Two, I discuss, among others, the challenging and supportive classroom climates. In this chapter, I want to focus not on the overall climate of a class or workshop, but on the continual interplay in any session between these two important ways of working with learners. When the emphasis is on the supportive side, we have a supportive climate; when it tips toward the challenge side, we have a challenging climate. In any session, some of both should take place for learning to occur. I first consider how we know when to do what. I then turn to discuss practical strategies for offering both support and challenge.

Knowing When to Do What

As I observed the teacher mentioned above, I thought about how many small and seemingly insignificant moments make up an hour or two of teaching. However, none of these moments actually is insignificant. We proceed intuitively most of the time. It is hard to consider each moment while in that moment. There is what has been called "reflection in action" (Schön, 1983), a kind of thinking about what we are doing as we are doing it and making important decisions as we act. Experienced and expert teachers do this well; it becomes tacit knowledge, something we can no longer articulate. I would be surprised if yesterday's teacher could easily say how he did what he did. However, I would like to return to the idea of *moments* in teaching to try to express this process. There are many kinds of moments; I have chosen just a few to illustrate how we can think about when to do what.

- There is the *unsure moment*, when a student tentatively expresses a point of view, when someone who rarely speaks in class ventures forth with an idea, or when people seem uncertain about what is taking place.

  > This moment calls for a supportive response. We need to acknowledge, praise, and confirm.

- There is the *anxious moment*, when someone is obviously flustered or nervous, when a student feels insecure or lacks experience and knowledge, or when a fellow student responds too harshly to what another person has said.

  > This moment also needs a supportive reaction. We need to soothe, applaud, and smooth over.

- There is the *joyful moment*, when a student has a major insight, when a wonderful new idea has been created, or when everything comes together perfectly in the group.

  > This moment, too, needs support. We need to celebrate, cheer, and compliment.

- There is the *blind-spot moment*, when a learner simply cannot see another way of thinking, when someone makes an assumption but does not see she has done so, or when the entire group ignores an important implication.

  > This moment needs to be challenged. We need to provide another argument, articulate a hidden assumption, and ask a critical question.

- There is the *confident moment*, when students are sure of their opinions, based on their experiences or readings, when people are convinced they are right even though a valid alternative exists, or when people have taken a firm position based on the discussion.

> This moment may also arise when a student presents a "right answer" from some other context. He or she may stifle other points of view. Of course, we do not argue with everyone who expresses a viewpoint with confidence, but this is a moment for challenge. We need to ask, "How did you come to that conclusion?" or "Why do you think that is true?" or "Do you think the opposing view has any validity?"

- There is the *authoritarian moment,* when learners cite an authority to persuade others of a point of view, when the continuation of discussion is threatened due to the introduction of an expert's statement, or when political or religious leaders are quoted to close an argument.

> This can be as simple as someone saying, "My father always said…" or complex as invoking a religious belief in a discussion of social issues. We must never offend or appear to be imposing our values, but this is a moment for a critical question or the expression of an alternative viewpoint. Our goal is to increase people's awareness of options, to raise consciousness, but never to indoctrinate or dictate.

How To Be Supportive

In Chapter Thirteen, I discuss the importance of authenticity in communication and good teaching. Authenticity is also at the core of providing support for learners. The more we identify with and relate to learners in an honest way, the more supportive our interactions will be. The authentic teacher also brings her experiences as a learner into her understanding of her students. To say "I remember what it was like to learn this for the first time" or "This is how it felt for me when I first had to do that" conveys a powerful sense of support through genuine expression. At the simplest level, we do not feel supported or cared for by someone who appears to be faking their interest in us.

Even when we bring a genuine sense of self into our practice, it is difficult to be aware of all the little things we do that are or are not supportive. Those moments in teaching, such as a facial expression, a glance at a person, a smile, a shift forwards in our chair, a tone of voice, all make a difference. Here are some ways in which we react supportively to student responses.

- When we agree with a student or accept that he or she has made a valid point, we support.

    This can be a simple, but genuinely felt, "Good point," a more detailed statement of how and why we agree with what was said, or a recognition of the reason for the comment even though we may not personally agree.

- When we recognize people's experience and knowledge by noting that others feel the same way, have had the same experience, or have thought about the issue in a similar fashion, we support.

    Various connections include other people in the group ("Sarah said that earlier in the session"), a reading ("That's similar to Coleman's point of view"), or a public or media interpretation ("I heard someone say that on the Ideas program").

- Acknowledging someone's perspective is always important. It is a way of saying, "You are part of this."

> If an anxious or unsure student expresses himself, we should take care not to overlook the contribution, even if we do not agree or the relevance to the discussion is not completely clear.

- Praise is always supportive, though it may lose its value if overused, or if that is all we do.

    > Saying, "That's really interesting, I like the way you said that" or "You've made an important contribution to our understanding with that point" not only supports the learner, but also encourages and inspires.

- When we take a participant's idea and elaborate, expand, and relate it to other ideas, we are being supportive of what that person said.

    > We are saying this is a good idea, worthy of further discussion and thought.

- If a student makes a suggestion we have not thought of before, this provides a wonderful opportunity to be supportive.

    > Students will glow with the knowledge that they have thought of something we had not considered.

- Similarly, it is important to recognize when a student or class has changed the nature of learning from what we anticipated or expected.

    > We need to let each person and group know they are different from all of the others we have experienced.

Not all of the support needs to come from the educator. When we create a supportive or collaborative atmosphere (Chapter Two), set up good discussions (Chapter Ten), and use group work effectively (Chapter Fourteen), we encourage participants to support each other. If opportunity is there for people to get to know each other and learn about their experiences and strengths, they will turn to each other perhaps more easily than they turn to us. Ideally, support from peers spills over outside the classroom or workshop. When people contact each other after the learning session to exchange ideas and buoy each other up during stressful times, a kind of support exists that we would not be able to provide ourselves. We need to do everything we can to facilitate this. We can:

- Encourage people to ask each other questions or comment on what is said.

- Make connections between people who share a common interest.

- Promote pair work and teamwork.

- Refer students to each other for assistance.

- Distribute everyone's e-mail address or phone number (with their permission).

- Set up a web-based discussion forum.

- Help people become engaged in group projects outside of class.

How to Be Challenging

It is difficult to be aware of our own assumptions. By definition, they underlie and form the way we see the world and, as such, are usually held unconsciously (see Chapter Eighteen). However, once we identify and articulate an assumption, it becomes open to debate. We can choose either to maintain or to reject that way of seeing things and thereby gain greater control over how we live and how we interpret our experience. We have clusters of assumptions. People usually strive for congruence; that is, they try to ensure that their beliefs do not contradict each other. These clusters of assumptions, about ourselves, religion, customs, social norms, and personal relationships enable us to understand and function in the world. Therefore, it may be difficult for us to uncover our assumptions or habits of thought in solitude. When, as educators, we want to challenge people to articulate and question their assumptions, we need to do this through dialogue between learners and ourselves, and among learners.

In order to challenge learners to examine their own assumptions or consider another point of view, we need to help them to:

- Identify their thinking processes.

- Question their own and others' views.

- Become aware of alternatives.

The teacher I describe at the beginning of this chapter accomplished this primarily with a good questioning technique. However, any strategy that results in a participant saying, "Oh, I didn't think of it that way before" is a strategy that challenges.

In Chapter Fifteen, I review a variety of learning activities, emphasizing their use in encouraging critical questioning. Most learning activities that operate at the level of application of knowledge can shift to foster critical thinking. For example:

- A role play, which traditionally gives students the opportunity to try something out in a safe and enjoyable environment, can challenge.

  > When people take on a different role from their own, for example, when a teacher plays a troubled student or a counselor plays one of her clients, then the activity becomes one which encourages considering different points of view.

- Similarly, debates, case studies, critical incidents, simulations, various writing activities, journals, and creative projects can all encourage critical thought.

  > A case study can incorporate a provocative issue; critical incidents can unveil hidden and uncritically assimilated assumptions. Each time we develop an activity for a class or workshop, we can include some element of challenge.

Mezirow (2000) writes about a specialized kind of dialogue called reflective discourse during which people attempt to justify their beliefs and interpretations of events, and come to a common understanding. By drawing on other people's experiences and wisdom, learners can come to a better-justified understanding of their own interpretations and assumptions. In Chapter Ten, I describe collaborative and transformative discussion, the process that can help people identify and question the assumptions that drive their way of seeing the world.

- Questioning (see Chapter Eighteen) is an excellent way of challenging learners.

  > We should ask people what they believe, how they came to believe it, what principles underlie their belief, what support or evidence they rely on, and why this belief matters to them. In so doing, we are encouraging people to reflect on and question their own experiences.

- In addition, we need to promote students' questioning of others' perspectives.

  > If students become skeptical of what they read and hear, ask for evidence, and look at the other side of issues, a norm of critical thinking is established.

- As teachers, we should model this kind of thinking.

  > We can present different ways of viewing each issue either in our discussion of the issue or through readings and other resources. The goal is to look continually for an alternative way of understanding something. We ask such questions as, "What would it be like if this were not true?" "How would our educational system look if there were no schools?" "Should higher education be free?" "How does technology change our way of communication?" "What would happen if the Internet collapsed tomorrow?"

Summary

For some teachers, being supportive may come more easily than being challenging and vice versa. It is important first to be aware of our natural inclinations in one direction or the other and then to be conscious of how we can incorporate both support and challenge into our interactions with learners. In this chapter, I identify some moments in the string of moments that make up a learning session where support or challenge are called for. There are many other kinds of moments, of course, but perhaps becoming mindful of these moments will help us think about the nature of our response to each.

To be truly supportive, we need to be authentic in our relationships with learners. Inauthentic interactions cannot be supportive. Being supportive means agreeing with the good points raised by students, validating people's experiences, acknowledging others' perspectives, praising people, elaborating on their ideas, and recognizing their unique contributions. However, the full burden of support need not be on our shoulders. It is equally important to encourage participants to support each other, both in the learning session and outside of it.

To be challenging, we continually need to encourage alternative perspectives and points of view. Most learning activities can be designed to do that. Especially important is engaging in the kind of dialogue or discourse where individuals draw on each other's experience and knowledge to recognize alternatives. Although Mezirow (2000) and others see coming to consensus as an outcome of discourse, there are many occasions in which individuals will choose to maintain their individual perspectives.

And, as I illustrate with the opening anecdote in this chapter, skillful questioning is an invaluable way of promoting critical thought. We need to question students, encourage them to question themselves and others, and model the process of always considering other sides of the issue.

Chapter Seventeen

Using Technology

The steady pressure to integrate technology into teaching continues. Educators who quail at the bewildering array of options and balk at high-tech talk feel guilty and behind the times. I approached my own first experience with online learning last fall with considerable trepidation, skepticism, and anxiety. I could not believe that I would be able to master the mysterious ways of an electronic system called *Blackboard*, let alone work with students without ever seeing them.

I not only survived but also came to enjoy the interactions with students scattered across North America and Japan, as well as the freedom of "teaching" at home. I felt able to develop deep and genuine relationships with people; participants reported they were able to be critically reflective and consider alternative perspectives through our discussions.

In this chapter, I discuss what technology can contribute to our work with learners, followed by some thoughts on what technology cannot do. I look at specific applications and some practical things we can do. Finally, I provide some guidelines for teachers working in online environments.

What Can Technology Add?

Just as the printed word and the mass publication of materials fundamentally changed teaching and learning by making information accessible, technology has exponentially increased our access to information, changed the way we see things, and expanded our opportunities for communication. However, there are disadvantages as well. For example, it is difficult to sift through the enormous amount of information to decide what is valid and credible. Keeping up with e-mail messages from students now takes up a great deal of time. But, for the moment, let us look at what technology contributes.

- Through technology, particularly the Internet, we have access to more information, more in-depth analysis, and more perspectives on issues.

  > We can locate illustrations, examples, and models not easily found in other media. Participants can complete learning styles or personality inventories online and get instant results, or they can watch the Ross Ice Shelf gradually breaking away from its home glacier. No matter the subject, up-to-the-minute photographs, animated models, and various points of view are available.

- Multimedia technology allows us to combine video, sound, text, drawings, and animation to show participants things they could not otherwise see.

  > We can exhibit processes that normally take place too quickly, too slowly, or too far away for us to access. We can show data analysis, graphing, simulations, or time-lapse animations. By projecting from a laptop or a regular computer in a "smart classroom" (one equipped with technology), we can show students

what we are doing as we are doing it. Akin to working through a problem on a chalkboard while the participants watch, it gives us much more scope and flexibility.

- A slick presentation should not take precedence over content and student involvement in the learning process, but multimedia displays can enhance understanding.

  > We can sometimes demonstrate different perspectives or interpretations. For example bringing in a guest from another culture via video conferencing may accomplish this.

- By mounting a simple web page for a course, learners have access to our own notes for class, supplemental information, or guidelines and suggestions for learning projects.

  > Students can prepare for class by reading the educator's notes in advance. They are then free to listen and discuss rather than taking notes. Also helpful is the access students have to post their thoughts and ideas on the web page.

- Technology makes it possible for students to communicate with each other and their teacher outside the classroom through e-mail or a listserv.

  > A listserv is a mechanism by which someone sends one message to every participant in a group. This provides support and may stimulate critical reflection.

- Perhaps most important, as distance education programs flourish, technology gives people access to adult education in a new way.

  > Through online learning, participants can live or work anywhere in the world, in the most remote locations, and be involved in learning sessions. Online learning also allows, to a certain extent, people to work at their own pace or at least to work at a time of day and in places that are convenient for them.

What Technology Is Not

The use of technology is not a substitute for teaching. A multimedia show does not make up for poor planning or replace participant discussion. A PowerPoint slide show is inherently no better than a set of good overhead transparencies.

As with any other medium or resource, the effectiveness of technology depends on when and how we use it. We need to ask ourselves why we are using technology and to weigh those reasons against any disadvantages, as we do in any other teaching decision. It might matter less that an online course allows access for someone in rural Montana than the fact that the face-to-face interaction is absent. Sometimes, the hours spent preparing a demonstration might be better spent meeting individually with students.

Technology provides us with wonderful tools and opportunities, but it is a medium, a resource, and a means of facilitating learning. It supplements; it does not replace.

Applications

What can we do to best use the various aspects of technology available to us? In making this decision, we need to consider our own teaching style and philosophy, our comfort level with technology, and the time available for learning how to use a new program. We must not reject trying something new because it is easier or safer not to. We also need to find out what equipment and technical support are available; both are becoming more readily available in most institutions, but we should still check before forging ahead.

I am a neophyte user of technology; I understand the fear of appearing foolish. The suggestions that follow include some things I have done successfully and other things I have not yet tried but with which I would like to experiment. Other resources provide ideas that are more sophisticated for the more advanced users of technology.

- Collect students' e-mail addresses and photocopy the list for everyone (with their permission).

    Set up a distribution list on e-mail, which allows for contact with all participants, or a listserv that gives everyone the opportunity to address the group electronically. It is easy to find someone who knows how to create a listserv.

- Set up a web-based discussion forum.

    This provides a place where people can post their thoughts, ideas, and questions, and where group members can respond. Most institutions have this capability.

- Go to the library, or take the whole group there to learn how to access electronic resources and look up library items using the Internet.

    Librarians are more than willing to show anyone how to do this.

- Experiment with PowerPoint as a way of organizing material and highlighting points when a fair amount of information must be presented.

- Bring in a colleague or other guest with expertise when unable to figure out how to run in-class programs.

- Find out what the students know.

  There may well be a resident expert on multimedia presentations in the group.

- Explore the Internet, looking for resources and software packages relevant to the course content.

- Given the opportunity, try online learning.

  Take a workshop on how to do it. Take an online course as a student, or just plunge in and try it.

Some Guidelines for Online Learning

Although there has been some research and writing on online learning (for example, see a New Directions for Teaching and Learning volume edited by Weiss, Knowlton, and Speck, 2000), this work is in its infancy. Most suggestions include standard good teaching techniques, what we already do in any educational setting, such as encourage students to talk to each other, foster deep learning, humanize the classroom, and so forth. The guidelines I suggest here come primarily from my own experience with teaching online.

- Keep personal interaction as a central part of the online experience.

  Because of the nature of the software used for online learning and the availability of material, it is tempting to load the site with information, material, and links to more information. In some subjects, it is necessary and appropriate to present information in this way, the equivalent of lecturing in a face-to-face classroom. However, if this is all that takes place in an online course, the educator's role essentially disappears once the course is designed.

- Suggest that students join in discussion forums and small group rooms where the communication takes place over time.

  > People write their comments, then return the next day to see who has responded. This interaction has the advantage of allowing participants time to think first and respond later with better questions, analyses, and commentaries. Many people prefer this to live discussion.

- Alert students to the fact that real-time chat rooms require excellent typing skills and move very quickly.

  > These forums may not be appropriate for some adult education settings. It is very frustrating to try to express a thought only to find that the typists in the group are ten thoughts ahead.
  >
  > On the other hand, with some careful planning, people can have fun "talking" in this format. The chat groups should be kept small (four or five people). Participants should be encouraged to wait for a response before going on. Entries should be kept short. We need to be sure to use each other's names so that it is clear who is being addressed. And the facilitator or moderator of the discussion needs to keep things clearly focused.

- Be aware that the absence of facial expressions, body language, and tone of voice can make understanding nuances difficult.

  > Without these to guide us, it can be hard to distinguish a light-hearted comment from a criticism, to understand whether someone is being ironic or sincere, or to know if someone is smiling, frowning, sighing, or yawning.

- Some writers advocate the use of symbols such as :-) for a smile or :-(for a frown or :-& for tongue-tied.

If everyone is familiar with this kind of language, it is convenient shorthand, but usually not everyone is. I prefer simply to say "smile" or "sigh" in words.

- Convey emotions as well as ideas.

    For example, we can write, "I am excited by this", "It worries me to think that", or "I'm saddened to hear this occurs." Once the teacher models expressing emotion through the written word, students will pick this up and do the same. We can also ask questions that pick up on emotions. For example, I might write on the discussion board, "Ralph said he visited the site of a concentration camp. Ralph, would you be able to tell us some things about how you felt in that situation?"

Since people are not in the same room together, it is critically important to make personal connections with each participant and encourage everyone to connect with each other.

- Establishing personal connections may take longer.

    In my online teaching experience, from early September to the end of December, four or five weeks passed before I felt that I knew people as well as I would by the second week of a regular course.

- A first step is to ask people to post a biography and a picture.

    However, more than this is required. Find out about the people in the group–their interests, their work, and their family–and bring these things into the discussion.

- Correspond with individuals by e-mail outside of the discussion forums to get to know them.

- Similarly, it is important for us to talk about ourselves, who we are outside of the virtual classroom.

> The students cannot see us; they need some other way to connect. We can refer to our pets, where we live, the weather, being in a good mood today, anything that makes us more human.

- Use names in every response to a comment and encourage people to link up with each other.

> All of the things that come naturally when we are with people need to be introduced consciously into the online environment.

- Include one face-to-face session, if possible. Then, faces and voices accompany the written words.

- Be aware that people may disappear in online learning.

> We cannot see them sitting there, and indeed, they may not be there. I found that people seemed to drop into and out of the course over different periods. With no regular class to attend, it is easy to put aside the course when life's more pressing problems come up.

- Keep in touch, send an e-mail, ask if everything is all right, check to see if the reading was too long or incomprehensible.

> There is no other way of knowing what is happening with individuals in the group when we cannot see them. We need to ask.

- Be very clear and careful about giving directions for activities, making "announcements," or communicating in general.

> I will long remember my efforts to get people to call me Patricia rather than Professor Cranton. I posted an announcement, "Call me Patricia." Two people thought that this was directed at them personally and that I wanted them to telephone me.

- Be careful not to dominate online discussion.

> It is not necessary to respond to every comment students make. I had to force myself to let comments go by and let people respond to each other rather than adding my input every time a message appeared.

- At the same time, it is important to participate fully, to be there.

> If a discussion is going on between two or three people, leave it alone, but if it starts to wane, come in and summarize what has been said or ask another related question. It is important to say, in such cases, "This has been a great discussion," or "I really learned a lot from reading that exchange."

- Let people know if we are not going to be online for more than a day or so.

- In order to adapt as we go, it may be important to learn just enough HTML to be able to make changes easily. Even though many word processing programs have built-in HTML editors, it is an advantage to be able to enter some text directly into the course software. To format this text requires using a few basic HTML commands.

> I bought *HTML for Dummies*, which served me well. Taking this approach also facilitates the process of students participating in the planning of the sessions (see Chapter Three) as we can spontaneously make changes in course documents without getting technical assistance.

- Be flexible; this is the most important thing that I learned about online teaching.

> For example, discussions take longer. I had originally planned for one topic per week, what I would cover in a regular class. This proved to be impossible, so I quickly changed the schedule for discussions.

Summary

The application of technology to teaching and learning is expanding what we can do. We can now sit at home and access incredible and often bewildering amounts of information. We can hear points of view expressed that we would never have encountered before the existence of the Internet. Students can participate in courses of their choice no matter where they live as long as they have a computer and Internet access. The directions that education has taken as a result of technology were almost unimaginable only two decades ago. However, technology does not replace teaching. It is a means, not an end.

In this chapter, I suggest several ways in which we can use technology in our teaching, from the simple use of e-mail through to the more complex online learning environment. There is a lot to learn, but it is well worth the effort.

For those inexperienced in online learning, it is perplexing to consider how we can facilitate learning, get to know people, and develop group cohesiveness with only a computer screen in front of us. However, this is possible. Based mostly on my experience, I give some guidelines for creating a good learning experience online.

Chapter Eighteen

Asking Questions

Unlike a skillful lawyer, I prefer to ask questions for which I do not know the answer. I find this not only more interesting, but also more likely to stimulate good conversation. It seems condescending to ask another adult a question for which we already know the answer. Why ask, then? Of course, there is a place and purpose for questions of recall, but in adult education, that place is limited. In thinking about questioning as a technique, I started with the kinds of learning we want to encourage. The purpose of asking questions in teaching is not to get a simple answer. Even when we are thinking of "an answer," it may not be the only answer.

> We design our questions to find out what students know and to foster learning. Therefore, the nature of the questions we ask depends on the nature of the learning we hope to see.

There are at least four types of learning.

1. We learn something new.

2. We elaborate on something we already know.

3. We transform an assumption or belief.

4. We transform a broad perspective or way of seeing the world.

These categories provide a useful framework for talking about questioning. In this chapter, I first discuss questions that help learners acquire new knowledge through memorizing, personalizing, applying, and analyzing. Second, I focus on questions that help people elaborate on existing knowledge through integration and evaluation. Third, I describe two types of questions–content and process–that help students transform their uncritically absorbed assumptions or beliefs. Finally, I explore the kinds of questions that help learners transform larger perspectives or ways of seeing the world. These include premise questions, questions that promote a spiraling of knowledge, and those which focus on the spirit, the body, and feelings.

Questions for Learning Something New

When a person has learned something new, our questions may focus on recall, or better, on ways in which this new information can be used.

- *Memory questions* encourage people to learn facts, rules, or principles by setting up a situation in which recall is practiced.

  > We must know something, that is, remember certain information, before we can go on to apply it or add to it. For retention to take place, practice is necessary. Thus, memory questions allow for practice and provide a check on students' retention of knowledge. Generally, however, more meaningful questions than these are preferable.

- *Personalizing questions* help learners internalize knowledge and thus make it "belong" to them.

Questions to further this process are, "What does this mean to you?" or "How would you say this in another way?" or "What words would you use to describe this?" When we learn something new, we need to interpret it, make meaning out of it, and link it with other things we know in order to understand it at a deeper level. In my work with graduate students, when they are beginning to understand a theoretical perspective or a new concept, they primarily quote the words of authors or others experts. I ask, "How would you describe this to a person outside of our field [your spouse, friend, colleague]?" or "Just tell me about it." When people can express the idea in their own words, the learning has reached a more meaningful level.

- *Application questions* encourage students to consider how they can use their new knowledge in other contexts.

    Application is achieved best through exercises, group work, and fieldwork, situations in which people actually do use the learning. However, questioning also has its place here. We can ask, "How would you use this at work?" or "What changes would you make in this procedure now that you have this new information?" or "Can you describe how this would come about in practice?" Any question that encourages people to think about how to apply the knowledge in their personal or professional lives is useful.

- *Analyzing questions* encourage people to study or separate the information or concept into its parts in order to better understand it.

    To know how a piece of equipment works, it helps to be familiar with the components of the equipment. To learn to write an essay, the structure and facets of an essay must be understood. To appreciate a new culture, it is important to recognize the ways in which it differs from the known culture. We can promote this process for our students in many ways, but good questions serve well. We can ask, "What are the components of this?" or "How is this different from what we read before?" or "How is this different from what you usually do at work?" or "Are there similarities between these two points of view?"

Questions for Elaborating on Existing Knowledge

As adults, we more often learn things that build on and add to existing knowledge than learn something completely new. Two important processes are involved in this elaboration of learning: integration and evaluation. We first fit things together and then judge the quality of the elaboration. The questions we ask can facilitate these processes.

- *Integrating questions* are essential when people are learning more about something or are elaborating on existing knowledge.

  > Learning must be integrated to become meaningful. It needs to be interwoven into the existing structure, otherwise it will fall off in the next windstorm. Integration, which is facilitated by group work, journals, and extended learning projects, is also encouraged by the right kind of question. We need to go beyond "How is it different?" and "How is it the same?" to "How do all of the parts fit together?"

  > *A questioning process* rather than one particular type of question best fosters integration. We need to ask continuously questions such as, "How does this fit with that?" and "How do these concepts relate to each other?" and "What is the nature of the relationship between these things (does one cause the other, or influence the other, or do they have no impact on each other)?"

Integrative questions may even help students make connections with knowledge they did not know they had. Sometimes a student will respond to a question with a surprised, "Oh, I knew that. I just didn't connect it."

- *Evaluating questions* take students to another level of elaborating knowledge.

These questions lead students to judge the quality of their elaboration. Is the knowledge helpful? Credible? Valid?

Valuing questions lead us to consider the value of our further understanding. Will it change our behavior? Increase our self-awareness? Add to our effectiveness at work? Valuing questions help learners focus on these issues. For example, a group of nurses studying to become nurse practitioners would primarily be elaborating on the knowledge and experience they have acquired through their work. Of the more complex diagnostic skills newly acquired, the educator might ask, "How is this useful?" or "How will this change your practice?"

Questions for Transforming Assumptions and Beliefs

We all have clusters of beliefs, attitudes, and feelings that shape the way in which we interpret experiences and see people (including ourselves) and events. We often are not even aware of these sets of beliefs. They direct the way we behave, and we act without thought. Someone who grows up in a home or a community where there is plenty of money may continue to spend money and accumulate possessions without much thought. Someone who lives in a community of aggression and violence may assume without question that acting aggressively is the way to achieve goals. Someone whose school experiences have consisted of listening to lectures, taking notes, and writing examinations will expect the next learning experience to be similar or, should he become a teacher, he may teach in this way.

When we do choose to question an assumption or belief, it is potentially possible for us to revise or reject it. One of our goals as adult educators is to help people become aware of and question their points of view, especially those that have been absorbed without thought and act as constraints. If, for example, a student has a cluster of beliefs about himself that leads him to think negatively about his ability to learn, we need to help him see what those beliefs are and address them. In different subjects, there also will be aspects of the content about which people have assumptions or beliefs that lead them to be less open–minded. A forestry student may have a set of beliefs that lead her to disregard environmental and social issues related to cutting timber. We should *never* impose our own beliefs on others, but we should encourage people to become open to alternative beliefs and better able to make their own choices.

- The first kind of question that helps to uncover assumptions and beliefs is related to the *content*.

  > This questioning helps students see *what* points of view shape the way they interpret the world. Essentially, therefore, content questions are of the "what?" format.

As it is often hard for people to recognize their underlying assumptions, we need to ask a variety of questions.

For example, with the forestry student above, we could ask content questions such as, "Is clear cutting allowed?" or "Are alternatives to clear cutting considered?" or "What damage do you see from clear cutting?" and "How many people live in or near the site?" and "Are the people who live nearby included in any discussions?" Depending on students' responses, we can continue with discussion and questions. Content questions need to be a part of a conversation, not asked one after the other, as they are listed here.

A colleague recently brought one of his assumptions about testing into consciousness when his students questioned him. School policy stated that students with learning disabilities should have as much time as they needed for tests. When he explained this to his students, they asked about the content. "What is a learning disability?" My colleague responded with a definition but indicated he would not ask for proof. Anyone who said they had a disability could have the time. "Why," asked his students, "couldn't everyone have as much time as they needed?" His response was a rather amused, "I don't know," which led him to give everyone the time he or she needed. An unarticulated assumption about the nature of testing surfaced and was examined.

- The second part of examining a point of view is to question the *process*, that is, *how* a person came to hold the beliefs and assumptions.

We could ask, "How might we resolve a conflict between citizens and industry over the clear cutting of timber?" or "How can we serve industry's demands for lumber and still leave a place for people and wild life to enjoy?" When the set of beliefs concerns a learner's self-image, it is important to try to uncover where the beliefs came from. In conversation, we need to ask, "Can you remember when you started to believe that?" or "Was there a person who told you that?" Or "Did you have an experience that led you to think you couldn't learn to work with machines?"

In examining both content and process, encourage all individuals in the group to work with each other to consider and question their points of view. Discussion should never become a one-way question-and-answer session in which the teacher questions the students, but rather a free and open conversation among all participants.

Questions for Transforming Perspectives

When combined, our assumptions and beliefs make up broader perspectives or ways of seeing the world around us (Mezirow, 2000). This is an orientation or predisposition. It is the way we see and describe who we are and it, in turn, influences how we see everything. If a person is a conservative, a liberal, a Christian, a Buddhist, a lawyer, an adult educator, an introvert, or an extravert, this constitutes a fundamental worldview. If I am a person who sees myself as a free-marketer, I will experience and interpret things differently than if I see myself as a socialist. If it is my nature to approach everything in a logical, analytical way, then I will impose that organization on what I do, and my experience will be different than if it were my way to approach everything intuitively.

Our perspectives give us a sense of stability and identity. When they are questioned, because they are so much an essential part of us, we often react with emotion—it feels like a personal attack. If someone questions my sense of myself as teacher, I may feel hurt and rejected or become angry and dismiss the questioner.

> So, when we alter a basic position, we are making an important transition in our life. Sometimes this happens suddenly and dramatically, perhaps as a result of a trauma such as the loss of a job. Other times, it happens slowly over time as we grow and develop. When my summer school participants come to see themselves as teachers of carpentry or mechanics rather than mechanics or carpenters who teach, they see themselves, and therefore the world, in a changed way.

The following kinds of questions will help transform perspectives.

- *Premise questions* address the very foundation of what people believe.

  > Essentially, these questions ask, "Is this true?" "Why do you think it is true?" "Why is this important?" or "Why is this so?" People cannot simply "try on" another perspective. If a learner sees himself as stupid and unable to learn anything, we cannot ask him to pretend he is smart. He cannot. Our questions must lead him to reflect on the premise of his way of seeing himself. Cohen (1997) illustrates this process

beautifully. He asks the student who sees herself as stupid, "Why do you give others the power to define you and your life?" and "Why do you define intelligence in this way and not this other way?"

- *Spiraling questions* show how each part of what we know about who we are is related to every other thing we have learned and experienced.

> Laurence Cohen did not just ask one question that led his student to change the core of her being. I suspect he took students back to what they knew, what they could do, what they had experienced, then asked a question that flipped that perception around, then asked another question that connected back to the original perception but from another angle. In this way, a student who thought he was stupid because he was not a doctor saw that he was smarter than the doctor when he could change a tire, and the doctor could not. It is hard to formulate what these questions look like, as it depends so very much on the person and the context.

- Finally, *feeling questions* ask about spirit and body.

> Transforming perspectives is not a solely cognitive process; it is not just about the mind. It is about the whole person. We feel different. Our essential spirit is changed, and our body encompasses our Self. It is important that people are aware of these facets of their learning, perhaps especially at the level of transforming our sense of who we are.

> When I teach such people as carpenters or mechanics who are becoming teachers and when they begin to identify themselves as teachers, they are changing everything about themselves. Where do they put their pride in their working man's callused hands? What do they do with their feelings of superiority based on their being able to do physical tasks with ease? How do they deal with their friends' views of teachers as soft and lazy? How do they understand the sense of vocation that brought them to teaching?

Summary

There is more to asking questions than simply asking the question. In this chapter, I do not specifically address the generic qualities of good questions: that they should be clear, open-ended but not too vague, stimulate thinking, challenge people to search beyond the conventional. However, I hope that these aspects of questioning are clear in my approach. I think it is important to consider what kind of learning we are promoting when we ask questions. I present a framework for types of questions and hope that from this framework, good questions will naturally flow.

Some kinds of questions focus on encouraging the learning of new things. These may be questions of memory, questions that help people understand their learning in their own way, questions that promote application of new knowledge, or questions that encourage analysis.

In adult education, participants are often elaborating on what they already do and know. To encourage this, our questions need to promote integration and evaluation. How does the learning fit into our web of experience and knowledge? How does it contribute to the quality of our thinking or our practice?

One of the primary goals of working with adult learners is to help them articulate and question beliefs and assumptions they have absorbed without much thought. To this end, we need to ask questions related to the content of people's points of view. What do they believe? It is then that we can help people understand how they came to hold that view?

When we examine the premises of our beliefs and assumptions, the potential exists for changing our perspectives, the way we define ourselves, and the way we see the world. At this level of learning, the questioning process becomes complex and dependent on the person and the situation. Essentially, we are asking the purest, childlike, and thus remarkably challenging question, "Why?"

Chapter Nineteen

Giving Feedback

I often receive feedback on articles submitted to journals, proposals written for conference presentations, or proposals for research funding. The reviewers, usually anonymous, may provide useful, constructive comments on my writing, but there is a norm in the academic publishing world to demonstrate one's own expertise through feedback on others' work. When someone writes, "It is obvious that the author is not familiar with the recent literature on the pedagogy of transformation," or "I wish this author had taken the time to read the article by Smith and Jones who provide a new perspective on this issue," or "This paper needs a complete reorganization to be comprehensible," or "It's too bad the author didn't think to check for split infinitives throughout this paper," I always feel somewhat taken aback and even hurt, and this after many years of receiving such feedback. I yearn for comments that are specific enough for me to respond to, and I wish people would not try to turn my writing into what they would have written themselves.

Even for those of us who are careful not to misuse the power that comes with the position of teacher, we must recognize the power of our feedback and be ever so careful about the words we use. Students need support along with specific constructive feedback. They need to be asked questions which will deepen their thinking without humiliating them, and they need to feel that their work is respected.

In this chapter, I first discuss informal feedback, the kind we give regularly and verbally in any learning session. I expand the notion of informal feedback somewhat by including notes or journal excerpts as a form of feedback. Second, I review several guidelines for giving meaningful written feedback on students' work. I comment on the use of personal interviews as a way of giving feedback. Finally, I discuss some difficult feedback situations.

Informal Feedback

Even when we are not deliberately giving feedback, students tend to interpret our actions and reactions as reflections on their performance. When we say nothing, they may assume we are disinterested. If we cut people off as they speak, they may believe we reject what they say. If we look out the window or check our watch, they may think we are bored. If we appear to favor the comments made by one student over the rest, they may be discouraged. Of course, we cannot always be conscious of how learners perceive our every move, but we must be aware of how people may interpret what we do and say in a learning situation.

Chapter Sixteen's discussion on supporting and challenging learners, contained several suggestions for providing supportive feedback to individuals, including agreeing with people, acknowledging their perspective, praising, and noting when someone has presented an idea we had not thought of ourselves.

- It is equally important to provide feedback to the group.

    > I often offer comments such as, "This group has such interesting discussions; I really enjoy them" or "I've never seen such a good balance of practical and theoretical points in a discussion" or "There are so many good stories and examples from this group." Of course, I only say these things when they are true. It is always possible to find some qualities in any group that are worthy of comment and praise.

- Give feedback when the group is not doing so well.

    > If response is lacking, we can say, "Everyone seems quiet today," and go on to ask why this is. If discussion is lopsided, we need to say, "We have to make sure that everyone gets a chance to contribute." On other occasions, it may be necessary to give feedback that points out that the discussion is straying too far off the topic.

- Never be demeaning. We need to be sensitive to the feelings of everyone in the group.

    > I once commented that a portion of the class dominated discussion, and virtually everyone in the group, including the quietest of participants, thought I was talking about them. There was a completely unexpected uproar in the group. One young man was ready to drop the course; he wrote me a long letter explaining why he felt demeaned by my comment (he was not among those participants who were dominating the discussion in my view). If I remember correctly, the group was in the "storming" phase of development (Chapter Fourteen) to begin with, but

my careless remark did not help matters. Rather than remarking on those who were dominating, I should have focused on giving everyone an opportunity to participate.

- Never make sarcastic or discouraging comments.

    I recently witnessed a young teacher telling his class of 40 or 50 students, "everybody did so terribly on this mid-term I couldn't believe it" and "the spelling, the grammar, what a disaster!" The students were looking down, shuffling papers, and obviously feeling uncomfortable rather than motivated, as was the teacher's intent.

- Encourage participants to give feedback to each other.

    This may seem difficult at first, but by regularly asking, "What do others think of what Sue said?" we can set up an atmosphere where people comment on each other's contributions.

> My friend Laurence Cohen, with whom I discuss all matters related to teaching, uses class notes as a form of feedback to his students. At the end of each week of classes, he writes detailed comments on the discussion, the points made by individuals in the group, and some commentary on the content. He sends these notes to students via e-mail. I adapted Laurence's idea last term and shared excerpts from my teaching journal with a group. They found this extremely rewarding and interesting.

Written Feedback

By written feedback, I refer to comments written in response to students' learning projects, such as essays, journals, presentations, or any other format (see Chapter Fifteen). Although not always easy to do, it is crucial that we respond to students' work as soon as possible. In part, this is simple courtesy; in addition, a considerable amount of research shows that feedback is more effective in promoting learning when received soon after the event. Here are some suggestions.

- Provide helpful feedback that is detailed and specific: we need to say not just that something is good, but also what is good about it.

  > Written comments should be of the form, "I really like the way you integrated these three concepts in this paragraph" or "This example is particularly effective in illustrating your point."

- Be clear and unambiguous as well when making suggestions for improvement or pointing out weaknesses in a learner's work.

  > I usually phrase such comments in the first person so that I am taking responsibility for the possibility I did not understand what the student intended. I might write, "I'm not sure I see where this is going here. Would subheadings help?" or "It isn't clear to me how these four points are connected with what you wrote earlier."

- Maintain a balance between positive comments and suggestions for improvement.

- Word suggestions in a way that is not directly negative.

  > "Next time, you might think about this or consider that."

- When a piece of work is outstanding, providing suggestions may be difficult, but a response is necessary and appreciated.

  > We can simply congratulate the student and suggest further resources of interest. Or we can suggest viewing the same point from another perspective, for example, emotionally rather than intellectually or intellectually rather than emotionally.

- When a student's writing does not meet expectations for what that person can do, still point out the positives.

  > I recently neglected my own advice with dramatic consequences. I gave only critical feedback to a student whom I assumed to be very confident and sure of himself. He was hurt, angry, and resentful; he withdrew from any communication with me for some time. Needless to say, I apologized and tried to reassure him about the quality of his work, but damage was done.

- Personalize feedback, that is, relate comments to what is known about the learner. If comments connect to something that the person said in class or something about the person's life outside of class, they become more relevant and meaningful.

  > For example, I might write, "This reminds me of the point you raised in our discussion last week," or "When you work with your staff, would you ever raise this issue?" Without some sense of relating to the individual, comments can appear to be generic responses we pull out of a comments hat and stick on a person's work. It is also helpful to use the person's name in making comments–write, "I really enjoy this story, Barb."

- Consider having criteria for giving feedback, though it depends on the situation; in some cases criteria act as a constraint on people's creativity.

Use criteria to help devise specific comments (and help the students in understanding our expectations) if the learning is fairly structured or technical in nature.

Do not impose criteria, unless very general, when the learning goals are more open-ended or emphasize the construction of knowledge through shared insights and experiences.

What I have found to be helpful in these instances, is that the learners, individually or as a group, provide criteria for their own work. They tell me what they hoped to accomplish and through my feedback, I help them to see where they have done so.

- Use written feedback to encourage people to think more deeply about an idea or see another side of the issue.

    I generally do this in the form of questions. That is, I might say, "Have you thought about how this might be relevant in another context?" or "Is this point related to the theoretical perspective we discussed in class?" or "Have you made your point as fully as you might like?" or "I wonder if there's another way of interpreting this."

- Use feedback questions to uncover how students feel about ideas, to connect to their personal experience, or to bring in a spiritual dimension if relevant.

    Here, I might write, "How would you feel in this situation?" or "Have you ever experienced anything like this?" or "Is there a spiritual dimension to this?"

- Encourage learners to give written feedback to each other, as is the case with informal feedback.

    Any piece of writing, whether it be an essay, book review, report, or journal, can be passed from student to student for comments. People find it helpful to hear from their peers, and as a bonus, they learn how to give helpful feedback–to be supportive and critical of others' work. If students are inexperienced in doing this, some guidelines are helpful. The guidelines given above could be shared with students.

Feedback in Personal Conversations

A time-consuming but extremely helpful practice is for both teacher and student to meet individually for a personal feedback interview. This meeting can also be conducted with small groups of two or three students, especially when they are working together on a learning project, but I find the one-on-one meeting to be the most meaningful. It is worth the time.

Initially, students may be anxious about personal interviews. Perhaps it reminds them of being called into the principal's office when they were children. We need to do everything we can to make the meeting as non-threatening as possible. Small things help, for example, calling it a conversation rather than an interview or meeting in the classroom rather than in our office. It is important not to sit with a desk between ourselves and the student. In my teaching, people evaluate their own learning, then meet with me to discuss their grade. Having the interviews in this context makes it harder to eliminate anxiety. Even after having worked with me for a term, I suspect there is some fear that another diabolical Patricia will emerge and slap them with a D grade.

Here are some guidelines for giving feedback in personal conversations.

- Set up a comfortable and informal atmosphere, including offering tea, sitting away from the "teacher's desk," and making small talk.

- Conduct the entire meeting in a conversational tone.

- Begin by asking people questions.

    For example, I often inquire, "How are you enjoying the course?" or "What's this group been like for you?" or "How do you feel about the discussions in this group?" We might also start with something from outside of class–a news event or even the weather.

- Ask about individuals' goals in taking the course before giving feedback.

    It is possible, for example, that someone had a goal of speaking out in class more often. If we know this, we can then comment on the person speaking out in class.

- Share observations about the learner's strengths and contributions.

    We can say, "I've noticed that you really contribute to the small group work" or "You are often a leader in the large group discussion" or "I've been aware that you always have the readings done."

- Offer suggestions for improvement with sensitivity.

    The way we express ourselves here depends on the student and our relationship with him or her. I often use questions or make tentative statements and ask the student to comment. I might say, for example, "It seems to me that you're getting lost in some of the jargon in the readings. Is that the case?" or "Are you struggling with seeing how this applies to your work?"

Difficult Situations in Giving Feedback

Teachers often tell me that giving feedback is not as easy as I make it out to be. How do we deal with the student whose work is clearly inadequate?

What about the lazy student?   The learner who tries terribly hard but just does not understand? What about the student who fails? How do we give feedback in these contexts?

I have trouble with these questions as they are posed; I prefer to reframe them in order to see them in a different light, and then to examine what we can learn about giving feedback. If a student's work is inadequate, what does this mean? It means she has not learned what we expected or has not met some criteria we have set. The next question is why might this have happened? Is it that the student is incapable of learning? Or is it that she was unable to learn this for some reason? Usually, it is the latter. Then, we need to ask what the reason might have been. Is it that she had not learned some prior material upon which this learning was dependent? Is it that the material was not presented in a way she could understand? Or is it that there were other things going on in her life that interfered with her learning? Or could it be that she has little confidence and self-esteem, and her view of herself interfered with her learning? There is only one way to find out these things, and that is to ask the student herself. Feedback, then, in this situation, comes in the form of questioning and genuinely caring about understanding what happened. It is not helpful or pleasant to give the feedback that the work is inadequate, but it is helpful and meaningful to help that learner see what happened. Hopefully, this can be done early enough on in the learning experience that there is time for change and "failure" is not the outcome.

When I am asked about giving feedback to lazy, unmotivated, or resistant students, or those students who have an attitude or demeanor different from the norm, I respond in the same way. I try to take the situation apart and understand what is happening. What does "lazy" mean? "What does "unmotivated" mean? Why is the person not learning or not seeming to try to learn? Is it that the material is uninteresting and irrelevant to his life? Is it that the material is presented in such a way that he cannot understand it, so he therefore presents himself as indifferent as that is easier than admitting he cannot learn it? Is it that he is in the wrong place or at the wrong level? Or that he has been forced into the learning situation by some other circumstances? Could it be that there is a personal crisis in his life that he cannot cope with? Again, I would give feedback in the form of questioning. I would meet with the student and ask questions about his interests, his learning, his goals, his motives, his life. My goal would be to understand what lies behind the appearance of laziness, lack of motivation, or resistance.

Summary

Feedback is critical if not essential to learning. If we think about trying to learn to draw in the dark or operate a complex machine with no guidance, it is easy to see how basic feedback is a necessity. When people are more self-directed, they become able to give themselves feedback, that is, become aware of how well they are doing. But even when we are quite advanced in our understanding of something, feedback is helpful. I send these chapters off, one by one, as I complete them to a supportive yet critical reader. I would be uncomfortable without his feedback.

In this chapter, I discuss informal feedback for individuals and groups. I emphasize the importance of never being demeaning or sarcastic in making comments. I suggest the use of class notes or journal excerpts as an alternative way of providing informal feedback.

Written feedback should be timely, detailed and specific, balanced between the positive and the suggestions for change, and personalized. Sometimes criteria are helpful, either set by the educator or by the learners. Written feedback can be used to encourage people to move to a deeper level of thinking or to connect to their affective responses to the learning.

Personal interviews are a remarkably meaningful way of giving feedback, even though they take time. They should be comfortable, conversational, and focused on the student's progress.

When I encounter difficult situations, I work to understand the root of the situation. I do not say, "your work is inadequate, and you will likely fail if this continues," or "it seems to me you are not trying very hard here." Instead, I ask questions that hopefully will allow me to find out what is happening and come up with ways to address the underlying situation.

Chapter Twenty

Encouraging Individuation

When we consider the major changes in our own lives and the lives of others, we are probably thinking about the process of individuation. When I left the rural community in which I grew up, and went to university, I left what was to me, a safe world. In my community, I knew everyone, everyone knew me. I was Victor Cranton's daughter, the one who liked to read so much. And Victor Cranton, of course, lived over there on that sandy farm, but he did all right really, considering his land. I had rarely been to The City, as we called Calgary. I had not watched television or even heard much news beyond the local reports on the price of grain. My first experience at university was frightening, exciting, and lonely. I was out of place because of the way I spoke, dressed, and thought. I had moved from one collective, the farm community, to another, a community of learning. As I learned not to say "ain't," to wear faded jeans and a sweatshirt (something we had considered appropriate only for work, not for going to town), and to express my opinions, many aspects of who I was as a person changed.

This process of separating from one collective, changing who we are, and becoming a part of another collective is one part of what Jung (1971) calls individuation. Other aspects include becoming aware of our unconscious, understanding our shadow side, accepting the presence of our masculine or feminine side. With each separation and regrouping experienced throughout our lives, we develop as individuals. Education must deliberately contribute to the growth of individual consciousness. If we do not develop a conscious sense of who we are, we can only imitate others and remain dependent on a collectively acceptable idea about who we should be.

Individuation does not mean the me-first attitude that seems to permeate our current society. "Me-first" is alienating. Individuation is a kind of spiral that takes us back to a better, more authentic connection with others, a connection based on knowing ourselves better. Teachers of technical subjects may feel that their curriculum has no place for this kind of learning. But I think no matter what we teach, we want at the very least for students to become a part of that particular learning community.

In this chapter, I outline several strategies for encouraging individuation. I group them into three categories: becoming aware of collectives, separating from collectives, and joining new collectives. I do not intend to suggest a linear process by this organization.

Awareness of Collectives   → KNOW EACH oTHER

To help people become aware of the collectives to which they belong, I once set up a very simple but effective exercise. I created several posters, each depicting common collectives, based on hobbies, professional interests, church interests, and a variety of other aspects I assumed to be relevant from my knowledge of the participants. People went around to each poster and signed their name to the collectives they currently belonged to. I asked them to return to the most important collective and stand beside that poster. This formed groups based on a common collective. People discussed what the collective meant to them, what values they derived from it, and how they had come to be a part of it.

- This activity can be adapted to suit different contexts. It is not necessary to use the word "collective."

  > Students in a trades program or a service industry can identify which facets of the career drew them into their studies. Are they a part of the helping-others group; a part of the working-with-machines group? In a workshop for managers or leaders, participants can determine whether they identify with the organization as a whole, their own staff or department, the people they serve, or those who buy their products. Each of these forms a collective–a group to which individuals feel they belong.

- Telling personal stories is a helpful way of understanding collectives.

  > Depending on the context, we can ask participants to tell the story of how they came to be in their current

career or their story as learner, parent, teacher, manager, nurse. Stories tell the tale of change, so as we listen to people's stories, we can help them to identify what collectives they are currently in and which they left to get there.

- It is especially meaningful if students can work in pairs or small groups to tell stories and help each other identify their collectives.

    Such an activity need not be long and involved. The stories can last only a few minutes. Once people become used to stories being a part of their learning process, it becomes easy to say, "Tell me that story" when an appropriate occasion arises.

- I sometimes encourage students to interview a person who is significant in their lives. This could be a spouse, friend, parent, grandparent, teacher, church leader, colleague, or employer.

    The goal of the interview is for the student to hear his or her story from another person's perspective. Often this process leads to insights about collectives to which people belong.

Differentiation from Collectives   → Know yourself

As people develop and learn who they are, they tend to look for groups of like-minded people. We define ourselves in this way. This is not to say that we need to or should isolate ourselves from our original family and community collectives, but we will relate to earlier collectives in different ways as we change. Meanwhile, the like-minded group provides support and validates our understanding of ourselves. We can help students with two aspects of differentiation. The first is coming to an understanding of the collectives people have separated from, thereby increasing self-awareness. The second is to help people move away from collectives that no longer serve them or perhaps even act as obstacles to their further development.

> In order to help people see the collectives they have left, I extend the poster activity described earlier. The students go back around to the posters and sign their names on the ones that represent something they left behind. Then they form groups by standing beside the poster for a collective they had left. This time, they discuss why they had separated themselves from that social group. What values had they not shared with the collective? Had some event led to their leaving? Or, what new interests had led them to new groups?

- Interviewing a person who has known us for a long time can help unearth the influence of past collectives.

> People remembering the same series of events will recall different aspects of it or interpret it in different ways. When we tell our own story, we tend to "re-story," that is to tell things in a way that better fits our current view of ourselves. A parent, grandparent, long-term friend, or a teacher or minister who knew us in our youth can provide an interesting perspective. Recently, by chance, I encountered someone who knew me as an undergraduate student. As we reminisced about those days, I was shocked to discover that he remembered me in a very different way than I remembered myself in those days. The conversation stimulated extremely valuable self-reflection.

- Examining photographs, souvenirs, and keepsakes from the past can help people recall important aspects of their lives and the collectives of which they may have been a part.

> In my course on adult development, I ask participants to bring into class a variety of objects that represent important facets of their development. As people show and talk about the objects they bring, others in the group can help pinpoint membership in various collectives. A high school yearbook may represent the strong bond an individual felt with his peers during adolescence. A photograph of a company dinner may show a person's identification with her workplace and colleagues.

In order to help people differentiate from constraining collectives, we need to design activities and hold discussions which provide the opportunity for opposing group thinking or social norms. Several of the activities described in Chapter Fifteen have this as a goal.

- Role-plays allow individuals to take on roles opposite to the ones they normally play.

- Critical debates lead people to argue against the point of view they usually hold

- Case studies or simulations can be designed to require students to look at something from a new angle.

As a member of a collective, we absorb the norms of that group without thought. Sometimes the smallest of nudges can make that unarticulated norm visible.

It is useful to analyze socially or professionally accepted perspectives critically and particularly to look for the places where the individual differs from the group. For example, in nursing education, students are first socialized into the nursing role. They become a part of the collective of professionals. It is equally important, however, to encourage students to examine that collective with a critical eye. Do they personally accept every aspect of how nurses are presented? In what ways are they different, as individuals, from the collective of nurses?

- In many Internet discussion forums, like-minded people gather to share their viewpoints on certain issues. However, it can be interesting and useful to participate in a forum where the prevailing viewpoint is different from the one an individual holds.

  > For example, a person who describes herself as a free market supporter might read the arguments made by people who are opposed to this point of view. Listening carefully to the other side of any issue can help students identify who they are, where they fit, and where they differ.

- Similarly, interviewing or listening to an individual from another collective, community, or culture can help learners distinguish with which aspects of each group they identify.

  > When I have different groups represented in a class or workshop (for example, Native and non-Native participants, younger and older adults), I encourage people to describe aspects of their collective in our conversation, and suggest that people work together in pairs or small groups across social groups to gain alternative viewpoints.

When learners have the opportunity to become immersed in a new collective, this can provide a dramatic way to differentiate one's sense of self. Most traditional professional and trades programs incorporate a practicum or apprenticeship experience where students work in a hospital, school, shop, or in the field with practitioners. This part of the program encourages students to begin to see themselves as a part of the collective of nurses or teachers or electricians and to differentiate themselves from the role of student or other collectives of which they may be a part. Outside of the apprenticeship model, we can find many ways to give students the chance to immerse themselves in a different social group–field trips, retreats, exchange programs, residential workshops, or even long-term simulations or problem-based learning scenarios.

Joining New Collectives

Individuation is not only about distinguishing the self from the collective other. It is also about regrouping in a more meaningful way with others who are more like ourselves. As we learn who we are over our lifetime, we can seek out more authentic and meaningful relationships with others who share our values and perspectives. We can also relate in a more genuine way to people who are different from us as we become less caught in the trap of pretending to be like the other in order to fit in. As educators encouraging individuation, we also need to pay attention to this part of the learning spiral.

When adults return to school, they are often in the process of breaking from one collective (changing careers, seeking promotion, moving to another community, leaving a spouse) and trying to find another spot for themselves. In one of my classrooms a few years ago, students prepared a large poster of a white and black spotted cartoon dog and underneath wrote, "Everyone needs their Spot." Indeed, they do. We need to help our students become a part of the collective of the learning group through support, discussion, acknowledging the process they are going through, and working to help them belong. Several of the chapters in this book address these issues (Chapter Two on setting the atmosphere, Chapter Six on establishing relationships, Chapter Fourteen on using group work, and Chapter Sixteen on challenging and supporting learners).

Outside of the classroom, here are some practical ideas to help students find their spot.

- Encourage networks and study groups among the people in the class.

- Refer individuals to special interest groups, clubs, or professional associations.

- Help people connect with others in the field or profession.

- Encourage students to engage in paid or volunteer work related to their new interests–places where there will be others with similar concerns.

- Direct people to relevant journals and magazines that can help them develop a sense of belonging.

In order to help learners avoid isolation or fragmentation, we also need to pay attention to how they can maintain a connection with past collectives while still being true to themselves. A woman returning to school need not give up her previous friends as a part of individuation. A Native person participating in a non-Native educational experience does not have to abandon his Native culture as he develops in new ways. Hollis (2001) writes of finding and trusting our inner guru. Essentially, as educators, we need to help people feel strong within themselves, confident, sure enough to trust themselves not to lose their sense of who they are as they relate to past collectives. Hollis says, "The conscious path of individuation means accepting creative tension of opposites, which inevitably involves a degree of crucifixion" (p. 118).

Summary

When we do not know ourselves, we try to be like others in order to establish an identity. We look to our family, community, or peers for a way to behave and for guidance on how to think. We run with the herd. And consequently we are dependent on the herd. If education has as its goal the development of critical thinking and full participation in discourse, educators must help people with the process of individuation. In our democratic society, the values of freedom, equality, and justice depend on the participation of thinking individuals.

In this chapter, I discuss individuation in three parts. We help people recognize the collectives to which they belong and how those collectives shape their lives. To accomplish this, activities can assist in the naming of collectives, stories can identify the tale of change that is life, or students can interview others who know them well and may shed some light on their personal story.

As learners grow, develop, and explore who they are, they differentiate themselves from collectives that no longer serve to identify them. I suggest a variety of strategies for helping people see what individuation has already taken place in their lives (which collectives they have separated from) and examining how they can differentiate themselves from current collectives.

Finally, I explore the process of regrouping, joining new collectives. We need to provide both support and practical advice. And we need to help people avoid becoming isolated or feeling separated from their past.

Chapter Twenty-One

Providing Meaningful Evaluation

Although participants' learning is not formally evaluated or graded in many adult education settings, in many others it is. In workshops, professional development sessions, non-credit continuing education courses, community groups, and self-help groups, to name but a few, assigning grades makes little sense. People participate. They learn what they learn. We hope they enjoy the experience, and that is the end of the story. We put our files back in our bag and head home. Should we receive notes from participants telling us how much they learned from the session, we feel pleased. If not, we realize they are busy people and do not think much of it. No one asks us to evaluate how much each individual learned.

On the other hand, when we work in programs or for institutions that give learners credits or certification, formal evaluation and grades are usually required. Somebody needs to know how much each person learned. Somebody needs to know which student learned more than another student. Somebody needs to know which student did not quite learn enough to be called competent. I always feel presumptuous in giving grades or determining how much another person has learned. I balk at having to select a B or a C or an A (or worse, a numerical grade) to represent someone else's learning. How can I know for sure? What if I misjudge? How could I not misjudge? In the last several years of my practice as a teacher, I have been fortunate enough to work in non-graded workshop settings or in adult education courses where the students are involved in evaluating their learning. Nevertheless, I realize there are many contexts in which instructors need to grade other people's learning.

In this chapter, I review three approaches to evaluation based on three kinds of knowledge we expect students to acquire. (In Chapter Ten, I use these same three kinds of knowledge to distinguish among different kinds of discussion.) When we are working with instrumental or technical knowledge, we can devise evaluations that are more objective in nature. When our students are acquiring communicative learning, the evaluation is interpretive; that is, another person judges or interprets the quality of the work. When the learning is emancipatory, student self-evaluation is necessary. Finally, in this chapter, I comment on grading procedures.

Evaluating Instrumental Learning

Instrumental knowledge is scientific and objective. It consists of rules, principles, and procedures that do not change from one setting to another. The law of gravity remains the same regardless of the culture we live in. The way a machine operates is consistent no matter who is turning the dials or pulling the levers (although there are people who insist that the photocopier breaks down upon their entrance into the room). The fact that instrumental knowledge is determined, consistent, and independent of context means that we can see whether or not students have acquired this knowledge by their answers to questions or their behavior. Generally, two people testing or observing the same student would arrive at the same judgment. It is for this reason that we talk about objective evaluation. On the other hand, as any teacher knows, it is not an objective measurement in the same way that a measure of length or weight is. There is subjectivity in the selection of questions to be asked, the way the questions are posed, and in the observation of any performance.

The ways in which instrumental learning are evaluated include paper and pencil tests with formats such as multiple choice, true and false, matching, and short answer. When student performance or the product of their performance is being observed directly (in the field, shop, lab, and so on), checklists of behaviors are usually used. To make any one of these test formats as objective as possible, several guidelines are important. For more detailed information on how to construct tests, there are numerous good resources such as Davis's (1993) *Tools for Teaching*.

- Each item should be based on a topic or objective that has been taught.

- Questions must be clearly expressed with no ambiguous terms or sentence structures and no trick questions or negative wording.

- There must be only one correct answer to the question (otherwise, it should not be tested using an objective format).

- For multiple choice items, as much of the wording as possible should be put in the stem of the item; the response alternatives should be equal in length and parallel in structure; and 'all of the above' and 'none of the above' should be avoided.

- True-false items must be clearly true or false and not a matter of opinion.

- Matching questions should include unequal numbers of items in each list, and each item should be plausible and grammatically consistent with the other list.

- When short answer questions are used for objective testing, they need to be clearly and precisely stated and have only one right answer, usually a word, phrase, or sentence. Longer "short answer" questions are subjectively rated.

- When checklists are used to observe students in action or to assess a product they have completed, each item should be clearly observable, refer to only one behavior or quality, and be answerable in a yes-no format.

- Directions for the test as a whole should be clear. Does each question have the same weight? Is there a time limit? How is it scored?

- If a question gets a class-wide, consistently wrong response, examine the question, throw it out, and reconsider the way the material was taught or how the question was framed.

- A variety of question formats should be used, whenever possible, on any one evaluation instrument.

- It may be a good idea to have questions that range over a variety of levels of difficulty, depending on the purpose of the evaluation. If we need to differentiate among students based on the depth or complexity of their learning, this is one way of doing it. On the other hand, when we need to ensure that everyone has learned a set of essential skills, we would hope that everyone answers all questions correctly.

- To make an objective evaluation meaningful and help students learn from the results, discuss the test with students as soon as it is graded. Invite students' comments and questions.

Evaluating Communicative Learning

Communicative knowledge is an understanding of ourselves, others, and the social world we live in. Rather than being based on scientific investigation, it comes from groups of people coming to consensus on how things are or should be. The validity of communicative knowledge is determined by whether or not informed individuals agree that this is the way things are in their social world. Nothing is definite, black and white, or "always true." What is viewed as good in one culture or group (monogamy, for example, or schools structured according to age groups) may not be valued in another culture or group.

Communicative learning is usually evaluated through students' written work, including essays, papers, and reports. As I discuss in Chapter Fifteen, there are alternatives to written work such as paintings, sculptures, collages, crafts, and other innovative and creative ways of demonstrating learning. Sometimes, students' communicative learning is also evaluated through a performance–an oral presentation, discussion, play, or dance. The evaluation is subjective by definition and trying to reduce it to objectivity only ends up diminishing the work. Unfortunately, in our learning culture we have absorbed the notion that objective is good and subjective is bad, and we have therefore tried to objectify all evaluation processes. I hope I can encourage teachers to see the richness and creativity that is enhanced through subjective evaluation. If we think of two poems, stories, essays, or dances, each of which is technically correct and therefore objectively equal, but then recognize that only one of these two is able to touch the soul or empower the mind, we can see that there is no way to capture the quality of the latter without subjectivity.

Good subjective evaluation is dependent on the expertise, experience, professionalism, and credibility of the educator doing the evaluation. Some guidelines may be helpful.

- Everyone involved, including the teacher and the learners, should agree that the learning is communicative in nature and therefore the evaluation should be subjective.

- The educator conducting the evaluation must be a subject expert who is ethical, caring, and dedicated to doing fair evaluations.

- We need to identify the specific qualities to be evaluated (for example, writing style, originality of ideas, creativity, evidence of critical thinking) and discuss these with students.

- Sometimes a rating scale, checklist, or other organizational framework is helpful in making sure that we pay attention to all aspects of the work.

- It can be useful to have in front of us what we consider to be an excellent piece of work as a point of reference.

- As I discuss in Chapter Nineteen, we must give students detailed, specific, and personal comments–both supportive and challenging–on any piece of work.

- Discussion and negotiation between student and teacher should be incorporated into the evaluation process whenever possible.

As with all evaluation, if it is to be a learning experience for students, we need to spend time discussing the results either with individuals or the group or both. In Chapter Nineteen, I advocate holding feedback meetings with each student as one way of doing this.

Evaluating Emancipatory Learning

Emancipatory knowledge is freedom from the constraints of assumptions, beliefs, or values that we may have absorbed from our family, friends, community, or culture. These constraints can either be related to instrumental scientific knowledge or to communicative social knowledge including our perceptions of ourselves. If I think that medical intervention can treat all physical ailments, this is an instrumental assumption I have taken from our culture. If I question that assumption and learn about other approaches to health, I have broadened my understanding and become free from a constraining belief. If I think that I am stupid, this is a communicative assumption I may have received from misguided teachers. If I question that and learn that I have gifts and strengths, I have freed myself to do much more than I could have accomplished while thinking myself to be stupid.

Emancipatory learning is acquired through questioning, critical self-reflection, and dialogue with others. It is personal in nature and as such can only be evaluated by the person who does the learning. You cannot know that I thought myself stupid and have learned otherwise unless I tell you. And you especially cannot know how valuable or important that was to me unless I describe it to you. Emancipatory learning is an opening up of possibilities rather than a process of coming to a conclusion, so there is no way to predict the direction it may take. Therefore, as educators we cannot set up emancipatory objectives or learning outcomes as criteria for evaluation. Learner self-evaluation is essential.

To encourage meaningful self-evaluation, we need to be thoughtful, caring, and supportive. We must genuinely give up our need to control grades and to have the final say; in other words, we need to give up much of the power and authority that comes with the position of teacher. I should note here that self-assessment can be the evaluation strategy for one part of a course (that part with emancipatory goals) and not other parts. When this is so, the power and control issue becomes more complex as we are evaluators one time and not another. Here are some suggestions for setting up self-evaluation.

- Students should chronicle their learning in a journal, logbook, or any way they prefer.

  > The important thing is to keep some record of the learning experience.

- We need to help students understand what is good evidence of their learning and how to present that to others.

  > Though they cannot predict the direction of emancipatory learning, they can see the journey in retrospect.

- Evidence of emancipatory learning should include a description of the reflective process, an indication of a greater openness to other points of view, comments on participation in dialogue, and a report on changes in attitudes and behaviors.

- Another person should validate a self-evaluation.

  > That is, students should describe their learning to peers, colleagues, or the teacher so that someone else can see and acknowledge it. This is not a judgment but a confirmation: "Yes, I see what you have learned".

- Individual meetings to discuss the nature of the emancipatory learning are very helpful to both student and teacher.

Some Comments on Grading

I have never met an educator who enjoys grading. Perhaps this universal discomfort tells us something about the system in many educational institutions to which we must conform. The purpose of grading is to give information to others who need to make decisions about the quality of a person's learning. These "others" may include employers, but employers usually rely on letters of reference and impressions gained in interviews. Grades are most commonly used by administrators to determine who to admit to further study or by those deciding who is to receive a degree or certificate. For these purposes, a simple "completed the studies satisfactorily" might suffice. However, the rationale for grading is that when only a limited number of spaces are available or when standards must be upheld, administrators need to be able to distinguish among the best, the good, and the not-quite-so-good students.

Until this system changes, educators are required to assign letter or numerical grades. When we are working with instrumental knowledge, a kind of false sense of precision is available to us. We can simply count up the number of right answers, turn that into a percentage, and then into a letter grade if required. Of course, this is based on the assumption that the tests comprehensively represent all knowledge in the field, and that the tests are accurate and reliable measures of the acquisition of that knowledge. But it is about the best we can do.

When we are working with communicative and emancipatory learning, the issue is even stickier. We are looking at the quality of learning, its depth, or breadth, or originality, or even the way it is presented to us. And to this we must assign a grade or, in self-evaluation, ask the student to assign a grade. The only way I have found to cope with this, and it is not a very satisfactory way, is to think of the grading system as a kind of rating scale. I think of outstanding work as the top of the scale, then excellent work, good work, and adequate work.

With this rather arbitrary continuum, I associate A+, A, B, C, and so forth, depending on the system used by the institution. This should not be confused with what is called "grading on a curve," or having a predetermined distribution of grades–a very questionable process. It is important not to think of grades as representing the amount of learning (for this we cannot do), but rather its subjective quality as determined by us as educators and experts in consultation with the student who knows what he or she has learned.

Summary

I recently interviewed an educator who had figured out exactly what his evaluation error rate was. He said, "Seven percent of the time, I am off by one letter grade." I wondered how he knew that. He explained that when students came back to him to complain about their grades and when he reviewed their papers, he changed his mind in that certain number of cases. Of course, only the students who felt their grade was too low came to complain, so he adjusted his calculation for that. I speculated on what would happen if he reviewed all the papers a second time or even a third time.

> Evaluation of student learning is difficult. We would need to be able to look into another person's mind to determine what he or she had learned. Not having that clairvoyant power, we rely on what a student answers, writes, says, produces, or does. The possibility of misinterpretation is staggering. Nevertheless, we do it.

In this chapter, I review three types of evaluation procedures. When the learning is instrumental in nature, we can use strategies that are objectively scored. That is, two evaluators would get the same results. This does not mean that the strategy itself is objective, only that the scoring is. When the learning is communicative, the evaluation process is subjectively rated. We use our expertise and experience to judge the quality of students' learning. When the learning is emancipatory, it is only the student herself or himself who can provide us with evidence of learning. Learner self-evaluation needs to be done. For each of these three approaches to evaluation, I give some guidelines for making them as meaningful as possible. I end the chapter with some subjective comments on grading.

Chapter Twenty-Two

Endings

It is the last class, the end of the retreat, or the last half-hour of the workshop. How do we wrap things up? Should we review content? Give people a sense of things coming to an end and allow time to say good-bye to each other and us? It is an awkward time. Some students appear anxious to get on with their life outside of the classroom. Others may seem sad that this time is over.

One of the best endings to a course I recall was when Walter and Sandra, two Native students, offered to close our session with a Talking Circle. We all agreed, and Walter explained the meaning of the ritual and some of its purposes in his culture. We got out from behind our usual tables and sat in a circle in the middle of the room feeling just a little self-conscious and vulnerable. Sandra said a prayer in her native language, and Walter performed a chant. He then led us through a process in which each person talked about the course and what it meant to him or her, while others in the circle listened respectfully and quietly. At the end, Sandra gave each of us a small, handmade dream catcher. It had been a special course. We had enjoyed the diversity in culture, age, and religion in the group throughout the term. This was a very fitting way to end our time together.

That particular ending worked well for us because of the nature of our group and the topics we had been discussing. In this chapter, I first review some things to consider when deciding how to end a session. I then discuss two kinds of endings–one based on the content of the course and the other based on the relationships among people in the group.

What Kind of Ending?

In Chapter Six, I suggest that we can establish different kinds of relationships with groups depending on our nature and preferences, the way we see the role of teacher, and the subject we work in. It is in large part the kind of relationship we have had with the group and the kind of relationships among individuals within the group that should determine how a session ends. If the relationship has been close, we need to acknowledge that in the way we close the session. On the other hand, if the relationship has been based on a mutual interest in the subject, trade, or profession, it would be inappropriate to suddenly become emotional and intimate at the end of the session.

In addition to that basic consideration, a few other things influence our choice of endings. Even if people in the group have developed close and warm relationships, it is not always the right thing to do to prolong the ending with a sentimental activity. For example, if people have been living away from home to attend a residential course or a retreat, they are likely looking forward to getting home to see their families. Their thoughts have already drifted away from the group and are focusing on upcoming travel and a reunion at home. It is important to try to read the mood of the group and make a last minute change of plan should this seem necessary. I have also seen the opposite happen. A group who has been focused on professional interests throughout their time together may start to realize how much they appreciate each other on a more personal level when it comes time to part. This, too, needs to be acknowledged.

Our own nature and preferences as educators should also be considered. If the teacher is the kind of person who is not comfortable sharing feelings, it will be awkward to do so in a last class. For example, a friend of mine feels she has come to a good ending when everyone becomes tearful and people hug each other, but this is uncomfortable for me. If the group is inclined to tearful partings, but the educator is not, it is best to sit back and let people say good-bye in their way but not step into inauthentic behavior at this last moment.

Content-Oriented Endings

There are several ways to bring a course or workshop to an end through focusing on the content.

- A lecture followed by discussion is a traditional form of final review.

- A conceptual map of the main topics and ideas in the course on which students work is an alternative suggestion.

I have done this by putting each concept on a separate index card and making enough copies of each deck of cards so that groups of four to six individuals can work with a set of cards. People spread out the cards and then try to place them so that the placement indicates the relationships among the concepts. Concepts that are closely related can be placed in a cluster together; those that are in a hierarchical relationship can be placed one above the other and so on.

It does not matter how people depict the relationships among concepts. The point is to discuss the concepts and consider how they are connected.

In one variation of this activity, I have suggested that people do this silently, each person moving a card as he or she wishes but without speech or explanation. When the card shuffling stops, people can then discuss their arrangement. Finally, groups can compare and discuss their different conceptual maps.

- A game show format provides another review-type ending.

  Since I do not know anything about game shows, I often suggest that the group design the format. I may consist of a panel of contestants, one or two judges, and people asking questions of the contestants. The questions, of course, provide a review of the content. The judges determine how many points an answer gets (it is best to have the option of several points to avoid black-and-white or right-and-wrong kinds of responses). If time allows, there can be more than one panel of contestants.

- Brainstorming the key concepts from the course can be a quick way to conduct a last review.

  In brainstorming, individuals call out ideas with no one allowed to question or comment until the end. Usually one person's idea evokes another related idea. Someone records each item on a chalkboard or flip chart until the ideas begin to trail off. At that point, a general discussion of the concepts raised takes place. Brainstorming can also be followed by the conceptual map activity to develop ideas further.

- Question cards can be used to end, as well as open, a session (see Chapter One).

  The teacher or the students or both write questions on index cards. Each person takes one or two cards at random, then goes around the room to find others who have an answer, opinion, or comment on the question, and writes the names of those people on the back of the card. This can be made into a game by seeing who can collect the most names on the backs of the cards.

- A simulation or role-play can be a closing activity in some situations.

  For example, participants might take on the role of key theorists representing the main points of view related to the content. A conference, debate, or professional meeting is conducted in which everyone stays in role and says only what is related to the point of view depicted. To make this more focused, set up a problem for the group to solve while each person represents one perspective.

- A simple debriefing of the course or workshop is sometimes a helpful way to end things, especially if the group is small and a good level of trust exists among people.

  For this, we can simply have a conversation about the course or workshop. What would have made it better? What did you especially enjoy? What are the one or two things you learned that have made a difference in your thinking or in your work?

Relationship-Oriented Endings

If we want to confirm the relationships among participants and give people a chance to express how they feel about each other, we can choose from a variety of activities or devise one that meets the needs of a particular group.

- A variation of the Talking Circle mentioned at the beginning of this chapter is one option. Even without the native rituals, the circle format with individuals sharing how they felt about the course and each other can be powerful in its own right.

- Recording personal reactions is another final activity.

  > Have everyone take a sheet of paper and write his or her name at the top. The sheets are passed to the right or left around a circle. Every person writes a sentence on every sheet. When they come back around to the owner, they contain statements from everyone in the group. One nice thing about this activity is that each individual also sees what others have written.

- Making collages is a creative way to end courses.

  > Ask participants to bring in old magazines, scissors, glue, and markers. Bring in colored paper and flip chart paper. People work in small groups or as a whole class if it is not too large. Each group cuts photographs, drawings, or words out of magazines and glues them onto a larger sheet of paper. Markers can be used to embellish the collage. Each item in the design represents some aspect of how people feel about each other, the course, their learning, and the group in general. When the collages are prepared, hang them on the wall for study, questions, and talk. Quite often, people bring humor to their creations. Feelings are always expressed.

Another way of creating a collage is to focus it on the contributions of individuals to the group. I give out a variety of colored paper, scissors, and markers. People cut various shapes out of the colored paper, and on each one they write the name of a group member along with how that person contributed to their learning. For example, someone might write, "Alice always asked the right question" or "Rick listened to me" or "Terri brightened my day with her contagious laugh." These cutouts are then glued onto a larger sheet to make a collage representing everyone in the group. If the group is larger, two or three or more collages work better than trying to get every statement on one.

Rather than making a collage out of statements about group members' contributions, the statements can be delivered directly to the person. To do this, I bring in envelopes, each with one person's name written on the outside. I spread the envelopes out and as people complete their statements, they put them into the envelope for that person. When everyone is finished, everyone receives their envelope. They can open them at the time or take them home to read.

Summary

I feel sad at the end of a course and regret saying good-bye to people with whom I have worked. It is important for us too, as educators, to have the feeling of a good ending.

In this chapter, I discuss two different approaches to ending a learning session. One focuses on the learning and the content; the other emphasizes the relationships in the group. Which we choose depends on the nature of the group, the subject, and our own preferences. The content-oriented endings have as their goal a review of the concepts in the session and the associations among them. We can use lecture and discussion, conceptual maps, game shows, brainstorming, question cards, simulations, or a simple debriefing of how things went to accomplish this goal. Relationship-oriented endings have as their goal the expression of people's feelings about each other and the learning process. Talking circles, collages, or any strategy that allows participants to write or say things about themselves and each other will allow people to say good-bye in a meaningful way.

References

Apps, J. (1996). *Teaching from the heart.* Malabar, FL: Krieger.

Brookfield, S. (1990). *The skillful teacher.* San Francisco: Jossey-Bass.

Brookfield, S. (1995). *Becoming a critically reflective teacher.* San Francisco: Jossey-Bass.

Cohen, L. R. (1997). I ain't so smart, and you ain't so dumb: Personal reassessment in transformative learning. In P. Cranton (ed.) *Transformative learning in action: Insights from practice.* New Directions for Adult and Continuing Education, no. 74. San Francisco: Jossey-Bass.

Cranton, P. (2001). *Becoming an authentic teacher in higher education.* Malabar, FL: Krieger.

Cranton, P., & Carusetta, E. (2001). *Teaching in a new context: The Renaissance College experience.* Fredericton, NB: University of New Brunswick.

Davis, B. G. (1993). *Tools for teaching.* San Francisco: Jossey-Bass.

Dirkx, J. (2000). After the burning bush: Transformative learning as imaginative engagement with everyday experience. In C. Wiessner, S. Meyer, and D. Fuller (eds.), *Challenges of practice: Transformative learning in action (Proceedings of the Third International Conference on Transformative Learning).* New York, NY: Teachers College.

Fenwick, T. (1998). Questioning the concept of the learning organization. In S.M. Scott, B. Spencer, & A.M. Thomas (eds.), *Learning for life: Canadian readings in adult education.* Toronto: Thompson Educational Publishing.

Freire, P. (1971) *Pedagogy of the oppressed.* New York: Herder and Herder.

Habermas, J. (1971). *Knowledge and human interests.* Boston: Beacon Press.

Hacking, I. (1999). *The social construction of what?* Cambridge, MA: Harvard University Press.

Hollis, J. (2001). *Creating a life: Finding your individual path.* Toronto, ON: Inner City Books.

Jarvis, P. (1992). *Paradoxes of learning: Becoming an individual in society.* San Francisco: Jossey-Bass.

Jung, C. (1971). *Psychological types.* Princeton, NJ: Princeton University. (Originally published in 1921).

Kolb, D. A. (1984). *Experiential learning: Experience as a source of learning and development.* Englewood Cliffs, NJ: Prentice Hall.

Michelson, E. (1998). Re-membering: The reutrn of the body to experiential learning. *Studies in Continuing Education, 20* (2), 217-233.

Mezirow, J. (2000). Learning to think like an adult: Core concepts of transformation theory. In J. Mezirow & Associates (eds.), *Learning as transformation: Critical perspectives on a theory in progress.* San Francisco: Jossey-Bass.

Schön, D. A. (1983). *The reflective practitioner: How professionals think in action.* New York: Basic Books.

Tuckman, B. (1965). Developmental sequence in small groups. *Psychological Bulletin, 47,* 384-399.

Watkins, K. E., & Marsick, V. J. (1993). *Sculpting the learning organization.* Jossey-Bass.

Weiss, R. E., Knowlton, D. S., & Speck, B. W. (eds.) (2000). *Principles of effective teaching in the online classroom.* New Directions for Teaching and Learning, no. 84. San Francisco: Jossey-Bass.

Weissner, C.A., & Mezirow, J. (2001). Theory building and the search for common ground. In J. Mezirow & Associates (eds.), *Learning as transformation: Critical perspectives on a theory in progress.* San Francisco: Jossey-Bass.

Index